The Author

Dr. Sidney J. Drumheller is associate professor at the College of Education, Drake University, Des Moines, Iowa. Active in teacher education since 1956, Dr. Drumheller also served two years as a full-time consultant for Basic Systems Inc. and the Xerox Education Division, working to systematize their production of curriculum materials. Dr. Drumheller's writings have appeared in numerous national educational journals.

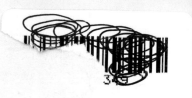

Handbook of Curriculum Design
for Individualized Instruction

Handbook of Curriculum Design for Individualized Instruction

A Systems Approach

How to Develop Curriculum Materials
from Rigorously Defined Behavioral Objectives

Sidney J. Drumheller

Educational Technology Publications, Englewood Cliffs, New Jersey 07632

Author's Preface

This *Handbook of Curriculum Design for Individualized Instruction — A Systems Approach* attempts to present educators with precise guidelines for designing and developing curriculum materials from rigorously defined behavioral objectives. These objectives, when inserted into the Design Model proposed in this book (see Foldout III of Appendix II) will literally determine the specifications for self-pacing curriculum materials.

Individualized materials which are capable of sustaining study require a comprehensiveness neither found nor needed in conventional classroom materials. The artist-teacher working in a self-contained classroom is able to continually diagnose problems, and prescribe supplementary study, because he constantly has his fingertips on the pulse of the group. However, when the class is going in thirty different directions with as many individualized programs of study, the materials must have "built-in" comprehensiveness. Such a situation creates one of the problems with which this manual will deal. The author has modified the *Taxonomy of Educational Objectives** by building

*Taxonomy of Educational Objectives: Handbook I, Cognitive Domain, edited by Benjamin Bloom. New York: David McKay Company, 1956. Hereafter this work is referred to in this book as the *Bloom taxonomy,* although it is the work of *several* authors. Material from this work is used by permission of David McKay Company, Inc.

into it a structure which can route a curriculum designer through a procedure, to insure a detailed comprehensive battery of objectives for a learning unit. The writer of the materials then can devote his efforts toward the devising of appropriate learning experiences to insure that such objectives are met.

The above problem is compounded when an effort is made to individualize instruction throughout an entire school system. Under such circumstances, if the study materials cover only a small portion of the avowed objectives, the school teacher will either be run ragged attempting to fill the gaps with individual consultations, or the objectives will not be reached.

Another difficulty arises when extensive sequences of materials demand a sizable number of writers, each working relatively independently of the others. If the parts are to be compatible, a detailed guide for each writer is a must. If educational objectives can be defined and assigned to appropriate writers so that each knows the behaviors he is expected to develop, the "individualized instruction" dream becomes a possibility.

A fourth problem involves the teacher who is guiding the student using the materials. He cannot, obviously, be deeply engrossed in thirty different programs of study. If, however, such a teacher had available a list of the objectives which accompanied each set of materials — and if these objectives were organized into a standard, familiar format so that the teacher could make a reasonable judgment as to where the particular objective was treated in the materials — then the capacity to communicate with the many individual students would be greatly facilitated.

The structures developed in this book will hopefully alleviate many of the difficulties inherent in the above four problems. The procedures outlined should be very useful to the classroom teacher and to curriculum committees in their efforts to design or revise curricula.

The reader is advised that capitalized terms appearing in the text are defined in the glossary, which begins on page 59.

Sidney J. Drumheller

Contents

                   (Reader is referred to exercises when appropriate and before he proceeds to new material.)

          I   The Bloom Taxonomy of Educational Objectives — Cognitive Domain

          II   Illustrated Model of Modified Taxonomy Structure

          III   The Drumheller Design Model

          IV   Portfolio of Objectives

Handbook of Curriculum Design
for Individualized Instruction

I
Needed: A Systems Approach to Curriculum Design

The role of education. Mushrooming movements advocating the use of computer assisted instruction, programmed textbooks or other devices which guarantee behavioral changes as a result of exposure to the materials fill many Americans with a fear that the next generation will consist of identical robots controlled by the state. They fear that once "ideal" behavior of the citizens is defined by those in power, an educational system will be programmed to insure the maintenance of the power structure and the subservience of the masses. Although such speculations have a kind of logical validity, they ignore the reality of the state of the science of education. After years of experimentation with teaching techniques, educators do not know how to teach children to spell, obey society's laws, respect the integrity of others and, in general, behave in a manner that enhances both self and society. Although science has effected great changes in many areas of life, it has lagged behind in developing techniques for changing functional behavior. Some day learners might be threatened by an oppressive educational technocracy, but that day is likely to be far in the future. Educators currently are threatened by problems whose only solutions lie in the effective application of behavior changing techniques that will greatly reduce the incidence of disrespect for the law, civil disobedience, racial strife and unemployment resulting from obsolescence of vocational skills.

Throughout history, schools have served a variety of purposes. They have served the state in building loyal supporters. They have kept children out of the labor market. They have provided babysitting services for parents. They have kept adolescents engaged in meaningful activities. They have provided a means for social and economic mobility. Currently in the United States schools are providing for all the above. Such functions, however, are not dependent on the effective programming of instruction but are automatic by-products of compulsory "education" where routine supervision is provided. Several studies over the past decade point out that the teacher-made evaluation instruments are primarily geared to appraising the accuracy of recallable knowledge and are seldom concerned with higher order functional behavior needed by the child or adult in his role as a citizen, parent or employee.

Many educators now realize that the school has served society well in its role as a cultural leveler and day care center. They feel, however, that the school has been considerably less effective in programming instruction to change behaviors to make the individual a more effective member of society.

The "Systems Approach" in the book title refers to the practice of using experience-based models of processes to identify the elements, relationships, and sequences essential to the production of curriculum materials by a team of specialists. A kind of systems

3

approach has been used by industry and newspaper and periodical publishers for a century but has only recently been considered in education. Curriculum materials, especially textbooks, have usually resulted from the efforts of an individual or a partnership. The individual usually worked alone developing his own ideas, only occasionally presenting them to others for approval. If the approval were not granted he would be inclined to seek another partner or publisher.

The Emergence of Programmed Instruction

With the emergence of programmed instruction based upon systematic sequencing of elementary instructional frames, the systems approach to the production of educational materials began to be viewed by behavioral technologists as an effective procedure for shaping behavior. When publishers decided to produce programs for a mass market that were based on discipline oriented performances, a systems approach became a must.

Research and development in programmed instruction led the way to efforts to use findings in computer assisted instruction. While the systems approach was extremely useful in the efficient production of printed programmed materials, it was *essential* in the development of computer assisted instruction. If these programs are not system based, information cannot be efficiently retrieved from the computer and the program breaks down.

The contributions that both programmed instruction and computer assisted instruction (CAI) have made and can make in the structuring of a scientific base for education are significant. Both the groups are building upon an evolving behavioral technology. Each group, however, tends to see his orientation evolving into the system which will eventually become the educational mainstream.

The writer is convinced that ten years hence both approaches will have established themselves in the emerging science. Now, however, there is a strong need for both a procedure that will systematically produce behaviorally oriented materials in a more traditional format that teachers can understand and that will systematically orient the teacher to the new systems approach. If the teacher can grow with the technology, he will be prepared to understand the new instructional media and use them effectively.

The Many Dimensions of a Systems Approach

PERT (Program Evaluation and Review Technique)[1] is a well developed procedure for systematizing the routing and scheduling of operation on a production line as well as insuring the quality control of the end product. PERT provides an excellent framework for guaranteeing adequate controls over factors within its domain.

This book, however, is concerned with another distinct dimension — design. A curriculum design system implies a referent model and procedure by which an individual or a team can, when given the desired terminal behaviors of a unit of instruction, break the objectives into teachable elementary components and effectively sequence behavior-oriented experiences to enable learners to reach terminal behaviors.

Two writers schooled in the system can, given systems oriented objectives, write compatible materials. Teachers familiar with the system can in turn diagnose learning problems of children having difficulties with such materials and prescribe appropriate remedial aid.

This book therefore will be devoted to the task of:

1. *Identifying the characteristics of a well-stated objective.*

2. *Defining a language for classifying, relating, and discussing objectives.*

3. *Defining a procedure for identifying all the objectives appropriate for a unit of instruction.*

4. *Defining a procedure for ordering or programming objectives into an education sequence.*

5. *Defining procedures needed for communicating specifications to teacher-writers.*

The Need for a Language Structure for Curriculum Design

Curriculum workers have long needed a precise professional language to assist in refining their methodologies and improving their communications. An

[1]Miller, Robert W. How to Plan and Control with PERT, *Harvard Business Review,* March-April 1962, pp. 93-104.

4

educational taxonomy might be the answer. The word "taxonomy" has been confined almost exclusively to the parlance of the biologist since Aristotle. It usually refers to that department of science concerned with the classification of plants and animals, according to their natural relationships. Only within the last decade has the term become common in the lexicon of educators concerned with evaluation and test construction. This is due primarily to the efforts of Benjamin Bloom and his *Taxonomy of Educational Objectives.**

Although a cursory glance at both fields would indicate that the word is being used in the same way in each case, one finds upon further examination a significant difference. The biologist is defining categories in terms of the physical, observable characteristics of the plants or animals he is studying, and in terms of their physical complexities. On the other hand, the educator is concerned with the classification of cognitive constructs or ideas. While it is a relatively easy task in biology to define mutually exclusive categories, such as bipeds and quadrupeds, or mammals and fish, it is extremely difficult to uncover equally clear-cut distinctions in an educational classification system. Cognitive constructs simply do not yield themselves readily to classification in a taxonomy category.

The following five qualities are characteristic of a biological taxonomy and would be highly desirable in an educational taxonomy:

1. A functional discipline is defined and divided into clearly differentiated categories. Mutual exclusiveness is the ultimate goal.

2. The categories that are defined are comprehensive enough to provide the user of the discipline with all the divisions needed for solving problems.

3. The categories are all labeled with terms that are compatible with the existing language of the discipline so that the taxonomy is an effective vehicle for communication.

*See Author's Preface for bibliographic citation and explanation.

4. The various components of the taxonomy are organized into a structure or pattern that clearly and objectively defines the relationships existing between the members.

5. The classification systems and the structure of the taxonomy make a significant contribution to the larger discipline that could not be provided for with the vocabulary alone.

Typically a taxonomy serves to order a currently chaotic field in a scientific discipline, through a system of discrete categories. To simplify the task of structuring a taxonomy of educational objectives, Bloom defined three domains of educational objectives: The *cognitive* domain concerned with behaviors related to thinking or the manipulation of abstract symbols, the *affective* domain concerned with attitudes and values, and the *psycho-motor* domain concerned with learned muscular responses. Although all cognitive behaviors have affective components, the two domains are developed independently. The primary emphasis of this book is the cognitive domain.

In 1956 Benjamin Bloom and a group of colleagues from the University of Chicago published *Taxonomy of Educational Objectives: Handbook I, Cognitive Domain.* Their goal was to establish a more precise meaning for those parts of the educational language related to evaluation. They used the term "taxonomy" to indicate that theirs was a classification system with a structure.

The classification system provides a language for the discipline. The structure describes how the language elements are related to each other. When an evaluator wants to appraise the degree to which a learner has benefited from instruction, the Bloom taxonomy, along with the descriptive handbook, provides him with a language and a structure to perform the task.

The Bloom taxonomy was structured to serve evaluation, rather than curriculum design ends. It is true that both are concerned with objectives, but the perspectives are different. Whereas the evaluator simply has to formulate an objective already present in the course materials, the curriculum designer must pull his objectives "out of the blue."

Several investigations (Gagne, 1963; McGuire, 1963; and Sanders, 1966) have indicated a need for the revision of the taxonomy, or a need for a special model of the taxonomy, to suit the needs of the curriculum designer.

The apparent reason for the limited applicability of the Bloom taxonomy lies in the author's insistence that the structure be kept neutral — free from any philosophical, psychological or sociological biases. While this is a noble objective, it is likely that the result of such an effort is a classification system, not a taxonomy. The strength of *Handbook I* arises from the fact that, in addition to the classification system, it provides a well-defined philosophy of objectives, numerous samples of objectives, and examination questions. The taxonomy itself is actually a classification system. However, when it is combined with the compatible supplements, it possesses the qualities of a taxonomy. Conversely, when the classification system is removed from *Handbook I* for use in curriculum design, it loses its taxonomic qualities, and reverts to being a comprehensive classification system and specialized vocabulary.

What the curriculum designer needs is a taxonomy for classifying objectives where the structure, when explored, will lead one to a comprehensive set of objectives, once a key objective has been defined. With such a taxonomy structure, curriculum designers will have a common language and a device for developing curricula that will provide a comprehensive referent for structuring learning materials—especially materials suitable for use in self-pacing instruction.

The task, then, is to modify the taxonomy structure and to outline a procedure for using the modification in defining curriculum specifications for writers and teachers.

The Bloom taxonomy presents a system for classifying educational objectives into six major groups, to serve as a device for constructing more valid and comprehensive examinations at the University of Chicago and (it was hoped) elsewhere as well. The handbook described the taxonomy, provided a rationale for it, and included several sample objectives and evaluation items for each of the 21 sub-categories. These latter were to serve as models for anyone desiring to use the taxonomy in the evaluation of learning programs.

The sub-categories are defined in Foldout I of Appendix II, but an overview based on that chart follows:

Educational Objectives: Cognitive Domain

1.		Knowledge
.1		Knowledge of Specifics
.11		Knowledge of Terminology
.12		Knowledge of Specific Facts
.2		Knowledge of Ways and Means of Dealing with Specifics
.21		Knowledge of Conventions
.22		Knowledge of Trends and Sequences
.23		Knowledge of Classifications and Categories
.24		Knowledge of Criteria
.25		Knowledge of Methodology
.3		Knowledge of the Universals and Abstractions in a Field
.31		Knowledge of Principles and Generalizations
.32		Knowledge of Theories and Structures
2.		Comprehension
.10		Translation
.20		Interpretation
.30		Extrapolation
3.		Application
4.		Analysis
.10		Analysis of Elements
.20		Analysis of Relationships
.30		Analysis of Organizational Principles
5.		Synthesis
.10		Production of a Unique Communication
.20		Production of a Plan, or Proposed Set of Operations
.30		Derivation of a Set of Abstract Relations
6.		Evaluation
.10		Judgments in Terms of Internal Evidence
.20		Judgments in Terms of External Criteria

The Cognitive Domain is made up of six major categories: Knowledge, Comprehension, Application, Analysis, Synthesis, and Evaluation. Bloom *et al.* maintain that these six categories incorporate all the educational objectives "which deal with the recall or recognition of knowledge and the development of intellectual abilities and skills" (p. 7). They have attempted "to avoid value judgments about objectives and behaviors" (p. 6), to remain neutral "with respect to educational principles and philosophies," and to keep the door open for the "inclusion of objectives from all educational orientations" (p. 7). Two basic assumptions seem to be held by the authors regarding the nature of the Cognitive Domain:

1. All learnings that belong in the domain are concerned with either communications or problem solving.

2. All learnings that belong in the domain require language either to acquire or to perform. However, neither of these assumptions is explicitly stated in the handbook. The Cognitive Domain, itself, simply implies that language symbols are manipulated in the performance of the behaviors defined by the objectives. If one wishes to use the taxonomy for curriculum design out of the evaluation framework of *Handbook I,* one's first task is to convert the classification system into a true taxonomy. This can be accomplished by weaving the categories into a fabric based upon the soundest psychological and educational research to date. It is true that there are dangers involved in tying a taxonomy to a theory because the theory will eventually outlive its usefulness. But there is a comparable danger of having a structure so neutral that it does not speak to anyone and does not fulfill any purpose.

The second task must be to reduce as much as possible the restrictions placed by the taxonomy upon the traditional language of education. And the third is to provide a model showing how the taxonomy can be applied to serve the specific end of structuring a curriculum.

A fourth task, and one not directly related to the first three, is to confine all objectives to a specific behavioral frame of reference. Although *Handbook I* was committed to this discipline, it often deviated from it.

This handbook is an attempt to accomplish the above without changing appreciably the original categories. It is intended that the resulting structure and model will be useful in serving the following ends:

1. The designers of curriculum materials and the designers of curricula will have a general blueprint to serve them in defining their objectives, analyzing their sub-objectives, and the weaving of the objectives into curriculum designs.

2. Teachers who use these curricula or curriculum materials, and who are schooled in the orientation, will immediately perceive the scheme in the tasks they have undertaken. Because of this, curriculum design can be considerably more complex and comprehensive than is now possible, as the language of the design can be communicated.

3. Comprehensive self-pacing materials can be designed, which are objective oriented, and do not require the constant supervision of an "artist-teacher" to make them work. A teacher who possesses the objective blueprint of the various materials used by the pupils in an individualized, instruction-oriented classroom will have a ready guide for supervising thirty children working on thirty different projects.

4. Teachers who cling tenaciously to traditional, outmoded curriculum structures and materials, because they are the only alternative to chaos, will find another path which not only offers order but also maps a route to adaptive learner behavior as well. Often the only deterrent to a teacher embarking on an innovative venture is his fear of disorder. The insights which follow can serve such teachers in assuring them that there are rational, more direct paths to legitimate educational ends and that they can play a part in charting the way.

II
Stating Objectives in Terms of Student Behavior

If one agrees that a clear statement of objectives is prerequisite to good teaching, good curriculum design, and good curriculum materials, then the problem to be concerned with is the best way to write objectives to facilitate maximum and efficient learning.

What are some current approaches for delineating educational goals? Most educators follow one of these approaches:

1. Instructor oriented
2. Activity oriented
3. Learning oriented (subjective)
4. Behavior oriented (observable and evaluable)

The Instructor Oriented Approach

In this first approach, the curriculum is typically structured in terms of an internally consistent formal presentation of the content of a discipline. The teacher may feel that an objective has been reached when prescribed materials have been covered. Some sample activities in such an approach might be:

1. The *teacher* will explain the causes of the Civil War.
2. The *teacher* will lead a discussion on "Lincoln: the Man."

This approach is most often used by teachers who want and need to have lists before them to remind them what they must do to meet some requirement, to specify activities they might add for personal reasons, and to suggest supplementary activities that may be assigned to keep students busy. The student is essentially an observer, usually passive, and often a pawn in the process. The emphasis is on the instructor *teaching* rather than the student *learning*.

The Activity Oriented Approach

A curriculum structured in terms of a sequence of activities in which the student will participate is typical of this approach. The teacher tends to feel that the objectives have been reached when the student has participated in all the activities with a reasonable degree of involvement.

Sample activities might be:

1. The *student* will discuss the causes of the Civil War.
2. The *student* will take a trip to a farm.

This approach is often followed by those who believe in the so-called progressive method. The emphasis is on the natural development of the individual, and the belief is that a variety of stimulating experiences will provide the learner with the necessary input to enable and to motivate later responses. More attention is paid to the structuring of the environment for learning than to the intended outcomes. The behavioral scientist does not disagree with meaningful activities, but believes they should be chosen *after* the objectives have been defined. Moreover, the environments and learning experiences should be chosen and planned to facilitate reaching the objectives.

The Learning Oriented Approach (Subjective)

In a curriculum based on this approach, the student is involved in intellectually stimulating, discipline-related activities. The teacher describes in general terms the concepts and skills the student is to master, but what is meant by "master" is not clear. Most objectives emerging from this orientation focus on cognitive understandings rather than on utilitarian tasks.

Sample activities might be:

1. The *student* will learn the causes of the Civil War.

2. The *student* will better understand the Confederacy.

This approach is probably the most common and is used by teachers who try seriously to restructure traditional curricula in the light of current educational research. The emphasis is on the student and his development, but the methods used are often traditional and arcane, and focus on the subjective development of the *mind*.

Little distinction is made between *knowing* and *describing, knowing how* and *performing,* and *being able to* and *doing,* As a consequence, teachers who use this approach lack the rigor of the scientist, avoid systematic evaluation, and seldom engage in controlled research. Adherents to this approach, however, constitute the group most receptive to the behavioral approach.

The Behavior Oriented Approach (Observable and Evaluable)

In a curriculum based on this approach, specific long-range terminal behaviors have been analyzed and broken down into their short-range components. These specific behavioral objectives determine the content of the curriculum and the learning activities to be included.

Some sample activities are:

1. The *student* will describe and defend Lee's position on the causes of the Civil War.

2. The *student* will tie both his shoes in bow knots in 20 seconds so that his shoes fit snugly.

The behavioral orientation of this approach lends itself to systematic study and controlled research. Adherents to this approach testify that it provides the key to the development of efficient and effective curricula and methodology. It enables the teacher to identify the learner who does not reach the stated objective, diagnose his difficulties and prescribe remedial measures.

To discuss objectives realistically, it is necessary to agree on terms. In this chapter *learning* is defined as: A change in behavior as a result of experience. If this be our goal, then the educator must be able to describe in exact terms what he wants the learner to be able to do at the end of the learning experience. Every objective is to be defined in terms of behaviors that, ideally, will result as a consequence of the learning experience. Hence the term "behavioral objective."

Constructing a Behavioral Objective

To construct a behavioral objective the educator should use the following model:

> As a result of this learning experience the student will:
>
> 1. (active verb) *Precise description of the expected observable behavior.*
> 2., 3., 4., etc., to follow the same pattern as 1.

This model can be applied to any behavior the educator would like to elicit. For example:

As a result of a particular learning experience, the student will:

1. (tie) both his shoes in correctly tied bow knots in twenty seconds so that the shoes fit snugly.

2. (identify) the oak and maple leaves in a pile of oak, maple, and elm leaves with 100 percent accuracy.

3. (write) with appropriate word or words when confronted with a definition based upon the essential elements in the glossary definitions with 80 percent accuracy.

4. (describe) the essential characteristics of a bicameral legislature.

The movement toward thinking of education in terms of learning outcomes or behavioral objectives has been growing for years and has taken on new impetus in the last two decades. Lucien Kinney (1948) with a concern for planning, and Robert Travers (1950) with a concern for evaluation, were among those who advocated the orientation in the late 1940's and early 1950's. It is interesting to note that the Boy Scouts of America have been stating their rank and merit badge objectives in behavioral terms for fifty years.

When an educator uses this approach, he can see the learning process with a clear perspective because:

1. He sets up learnings to be emphasized based on a philosophy and a chosen set of objectives.

2. He selects methods to be used to effect learning.

3. He does not feel defensive in terms of the philosophy, objectives, and methodology, because the student's behavior shows results.

4. He continually asks such questions as: Was this topic or objective worth the emphasis it was given? Is this objective worth evaluating? How should I weight these various objective emphases in the evaluation instrument? Can we expect the learner to reach an avowed objective considering the method that was used? Will this proposed test item actually serve to measure the learner's success in reaching the desired objective?

The evaluator especially must seek order in the learning process and reflect on ways to make the process more efficient. It is ironic that, in practice, his culminating role in the process sharpens his perspective, but the opportunity to apply his insights to make learning more efficient and effective by this time no longer exists.

Objectives and philosophy determine the methods used in instruction and evaluation. In this book, *philosophy* is used to mean the educator's unique set of beliefs and values that he uses as criteria in making educational decisions.[2]

In constructing objectives from the evaluation point of view, one finds that these are nearly identical with test items, and examinations are almost in final form when these objectives have been described in detail. The selection and presentation of the learning experiences then become the final steps in the process, except for the actual administration of the final evaluation instrument. The substance of such a learning experience has already been well structured by the defined behavior oriented objectives.

Classification of Behavioral Objectives

Objectives can serve many masters. Under the general heading of *objectives* are two exclusive classifications, each divided into the same four sub-categories. The chart on page 12 outlines the classification structure.

It is hoped that the reader, when examining this chart, will understand that the behavioral orientation has more than limited application in stating educational objectives. The chart also provides a simple language for describing the functional role of objectives in the educational process. It may also provide a useful referent for appraising the balance in a set of objectives.

What are some examples of behaviors and the differences between an "ends" (terminal) behavior and a "means" (transitional) behavior? In learning to swim, a child often uses water wings to give him the courage to take the swimming position. Assuming a swimming position using water wings is a transitional, or *means,* behavior. Once the child is swimming (the terminal behavior), the water wings (means) are no longer necessary. Swimming without artificial support is the desired terminal objective; it is reached, however, through a transitional objective.

[2]It may be pointed out that a major philosophical position has already been claimed — behaviorism. When one commits himself to this behaviorally oriented position, many educational goals and methods are no longer appropriate.

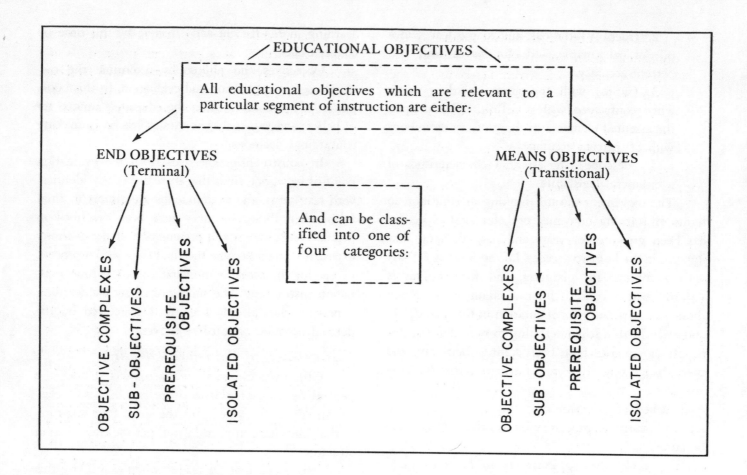

EDUCATIONAL OBJECTIVES

All educational objectives which are relevant to a particular segment of instruction are either:

END OBJECTIVES
(Terminal)

MEANS OBJECTIVES
(Transitional)

And can be classified into one of four categories:

OBJECTIVE COMPLEXES
SUB - OBJECTIVES
PREREQUISITE OBJECTIVES
ISOLATED OBJECTIVES

OBJECTIVE COMPLEXES
SUB - OBJECTIVES
PREREQUISITE OBJECTIVES
ISOLATED OBJECTIVES

A music teacher may instruct a beginning student to recognize notes on the grand staff by means of sentences, each word denoting a key. The student learns to recite "All cows eat grass," or "Every good boy does fine," counts up the proper spaces or lines, and finds the note. Learning such sentences is transitional behavior. Once the student learns that he can simply look at a note and reproduce it on an instrument, he no longer needs or uses the clue sentences. The terminal behavior in this instance is recognizing the note and playing it, without intermediate clues.

In the above chart, the four sub-objectives under "ends" and "means" are identical. In this manual, however, the author will deal only with objectives that are terminal or "ends." One can classify his objectives whenever he needs to by referring to the chart. For example, to discriminate between the four sub-categories described above, consider a fifth-grade teacher who is concerned with instructing his class in the conventional multiplication of simple fractions. Such objectives would fit into the categories as follows:

The (terminal) objective complexes deal with a few specific functional behaviors upon which the teacher will focus instruction. "Complexes" mean that the objective will be further sub-divided for instructional purposes. In this example it is possible to state one terminal behavior objective: The student will multiply any two fractions whose numerators and denominators are less than 100 and reduce these fractions to lowest terms, without error.

The terminal sub-objectives come when larger terminal behaviors are broken down into simpler ones. A few such sub-objectives might be:

1. The student will set up the problem in the following format:

$$\frac{(\quad\quad)}{(\quad\quad)} \times \frac{(\quad\quad)}{(\quad\quad)} = \frac{(\quad\quad)}{(\quad\quad)}$$

2. The student will record the product of the numerators in the numerator of the answer.

3. The student will record the product of the denominators in the denominator of the answer.

4. The student will reduce the answer to its lowest terms.

Isolated objectives are often included in the sub-objective category, but are not essential to the attainment of any terminal complex. They are simply "nice to know" elements that have often been labeled as "musts" by curriculum writers and teachers and attached to a terminal complex. Affixed to a unit on fractions might be the following: "The student will recall that the Babylonians used simple fractional notations over 4000 years ago." Such an objective may be classified as "transitional" if it stimulates interest in the terminal behavior, but is not a "must." Educators vary widely in their opinions of what a literate person should know.

Prerequisite objectives relate to specific behaviors such as skills, attitudes or knowledge. The achievement of these behaviors is prerequisite and essential to the segment of learning experiences relating to the terminal behavior objectives. When certain behaviors are prerequisite to a unit, they are usually the terminal objectives of a preceding unit. Students, however may need some relearning and practice to acquire the desired level of proficiency. Such prerequisite behaviors may be related to motivation, interest, vocabulary, facts, skills, and so forth. A few prerequisite behavioral objectives for the unit on fractions might be:

1. The student will perform the overt activities prescribed by the classroom teacher or in the supplementary curriculum materials. (An affective objective.)

2. The student will ask pertinent questions when he is unable to perform a prescribed task.

3. The student will multiply two-place whole numbers without error.

4. The student will define the following terms: numerator, denominator, fraction, multiply, reduce to lowest terms, etc.

The classification given to an objective depends not only upon what the educator using the curriculum or materials considers to be the terminal behavior, but also upon the level of instruction. This classifica-tion system, while helpful in providing the teacher with a perspective at a particular moment, is not meant to classify an objective permanently. In Chapter IV, a curriculum model will be developed that focuses upon a unit of instruction, so that within the confines of the unit, this classification structure will be stable and consistent.

Stating Behavioral Objectives Adequately

In evaluating the adequacy of a behavioral objective, the educator must consider the following six characteristics. Endemic to these criteria is a premise of the behaviorally oriented: An objective has no place in a curriculum if it cannot be evaluated with a considerable degree of validity. Claims and counterclaims have been made for educational philosophies, methods, and techniques since antiquity, alleging spectacular results with no evidence to substantiate the assertions. Reaching for objectives without planning for evaluating attainment is like going to the moon without planning how to get back. Periodic evaluation has a sobering effect on a teacher, and one committed to evaluating his objectives is forced to keep at least one foot on the ground.

The following are offered as characteristics of well-stated behavioral objectives:

1. The statement describes what the learner will be able to do as a result of the learning experience.

2. The essential characteristics of the desired behavior are explicitly stated.

3. The statement clearly specifies the conditions under which the learner will perform the behavior.

4. The behavior required is within the ability level and the development level of the learner.

5. The behavior is observable.

6. The behavior can be evaluated.

Using the above criteria, one might evaluate an objective stated earlier in this chapter. "As a result of the learning experience the first-grade student will tie both shoes in twenty seconds in correctly tied bow knots so that the shoes fit snugly."

Criterion 1 demands that the objective be phrased in terms of expected pupil behavior. *The student will tie his shoes.*

Criterion 2 demands that the essential characteristics of the desired behaviors be explicitly stated. The phrases, *correctly tied in bow knots* and *fit snugly,* define the characteristics.

Criterion 3 demands that the conditions under which the student is to perform the task be precisely stated. *A twenty-second time limit* has been defined.

It could also be stated that the shoes are to be loosely laced, on the feet and free from knots. In describing some objectives, one might add such factors as wind velocity, degree of hostility of listeners and amount of background noise. Factors such as these are extremely important in determining the procedures that must be used in the learning process if the objective is to be reached. A writer or a teacher who deals with specifics such as these has guidelines for designing effective learning procedures.

Criterion 4 demands that the objectives be reasonable, and it seems reasonable that *a first-grader should be able to tie his shoes.* However, if this objective were proposed for nursery school children or for first-graders with cerebral palsy, the criterion might not be met. The teacher might decide that grouping for instruction, or individualized instruction, would be necessary.

Criterion 5 asks that an individual other than the learner be able to observe the behavior. If an objective is stated in such forms as: "The student will have a better understanding of how to tie his shoes," or "The student will know how to tie his shoes," it does not meet the criterion. One cannot observe *a better understanding* or *knowing.* A student might know what to do, yet be unable to do it. Unless the teacher asks students to act, he has no proof whether they have learned or not.

Criterion 6 demands that the objective specify some criteria by which the learned behavior can be evaluated. In the objective being discussed, it is implied that the child will be asked to tie his shoes immediately following the learning period or at some future time.

In this instance, the evaluation tests *yes* or *no:*

Did the student reach the objective? When an educator is concerned with the gradual acquisition of skills by the student, the question "Can we evaluate?" becomes crucial. When one is considering legibility of handwriting, reading comprehension, writing style, correct English usage in writing or speaking, and other skills that do not have clearly definable points of achievement, it is often difficult to meet Criterion 6.

Two procedures commonly used are:

1. Administration of an evaluation instrument that yields a numerical score from which development norms can be derived. (A student might answer 23 items correctly on a reading comprehension test, giving him a score typical of a child halfway through the fourth grade.)

2. Comparison of a learner's performance on a task (usually a written communication) with three to seven models of typical performances at different developmental levels. For example, legibility in handwriting is determined (as in the Ayers' Scale[3]) by the evaluator's matching a student's handwriting performance on the "Gettysburg Address" to models of typical grade-level performance on the same task — a subjective evaluation.

Measurement instruments that show precise graduations of skill acquisition are usually quite difficult and costly to develop. Criterion 6 asks that the designer of objectives exercise caution in stating objectives in such broad terms that evaluation instruments are unavailable or impractical to construct. It seems important that educators who are behavior oriented make a major effort to create the instruments needed for evaluation in crucial areas.

This chapter has focused upon the question "What is the nature of an educational objective which provides sufficient direction for the effective structuring of curriculum materials, classroom teaching and evaluation procedures?" It was concluded that the behaviorally stated objective equips the educator with an optimum structure when it fulfills the following requirements:

[3] Ayers, Leonard P. *Ayers' Measuring Scale for Handwriting.* (Gettysburg Edition). New York: Russell Sage Foundation.

It is phrased in terms of expected pupil behavior.

It explicitly describes the expected behavior.

It explicitly describes the conditions under which the behavior can be expected.

It suggests an observation medium.

It suggests an evaluation procedure.

It defines behaviors which can be realistically expected of the learner.

Educational objectives can be classified as terminal or transitional and further subclassified as behavior complexes, sub-objectives, prerequisite objectives and isolated objectives according to the function they serve in the development of a complex set of behaviors.

The exercises in Appendix I will serve to develop a functional competence in making the discriminations described above. This level of mastery, however, is not essential to the comprehension of the concept developed in subsequent chapters.

III
Identifying Learning Outcomes

In this chapter the structure of the Bloom taxonomy will be modified to provide guidelines for identifying the terminal *sub*-objectives of a unit once the terminal objectives have been identified. The chart on page 29 presents an overview of this modified taxonomy, while Foldout II[4] in Appendix II portrays the taxonomy, with sample objectives for each taxonomy category. *It is essential that the reader understand the taxonomy* to master the later concepts because:

    1. It provides a precise language for use in discussing objectives.

    2. It provides functional categories for use in classifying objectives.

    3. It provides a structure that shows the relationships existing between the objectives of an objective complex.

    4. It provides a structure for use in identifying sub-objectives appropriate to the development of complex behaviors.

    5. It classifies derived objectives so that they can be integrated into a *curriculum design model* (described in the next chapter) to structure a curriculum.

[4]The foldouts summarize the major structures presented in the text, and once the reader has mastered them, he can merely refer to the foldouts assembled in the appendix to reorient himself to the structures. The foldouts can be left open when reading.

The names and numbers of the categories are identical to Bloom's, but definitions have been somewhat modified. The six major categories are listed in the left-hand column in the chart on page 29, and tend to increase in complexity as the numbers increase. These categories classify rather discretely the cognitive objectives used in schools today.

In this taxonomy, Application (3.0) provides the focus for nearly all the other categories. Application objectives require the development of functional, useful behaviors and, in most cases, are complex. When Application objectives are analyzed for component objectives, the elements belong to one or more of the five remaining categories.

Knowledge (1.0) is usually basic to the performance of involved, complex behaviors. By Knowledge, the author means recallable symbolic remnants of past experiences that are needed to make an Application response. A Knowledge objective asks the learner to recall information either with, or without, understanding.

Comprehension (2.0) objectives specify the degree to which the learner is to be able to manipulate meaningfully the Knowledge elements.

The higher level objectives are needed when the Application tasks are difficult. Analysis (4.0) objectives center on behaviors that help the learner to identify relevant Knowledge that applies to the performance of an Application task. Synthesis (5.0) objectives center on behaviors that help the learner to combine Knowledge elements in an appropriate fashion to perform an Application task. Evaluation (6.0) objectives center on behaviors that help the learner appraise the adequacy of a performance of an Application task performed by himself either overtly or covertly or by another.

1.0 KNOWLEDGE

(Development of ability to recall appropriate information, with or without comprehension)

The learner will verbally recall:

KNOWL-EDGE OF SPE-CIFICS		KNOWLEDGE OF WAYS & MEANS OF DEALING WITH SPECIFICS					KNOWLEDGE OF UNIVERSALS & ABSTRACTIONS IN A FIELD	
1.11 Knowledge of terms	1.12 Knowledge of specific facts	1.21 Knowledge of conventions	1.22 Knowledge of trends & sequences	1.23 Knowledge of classifications & categories	1.24 Knowledge of criteria	1.25 Knowledge of methodology	1.31 Knowledge of principles & generalizations	1.32 Knowledge of theories and structures

KNOWLEDGE (1.0) OBJECTIVE CELLS

The Knowledge category includes objectives concerned with the learner's recall of appropriate information, with or without comprehension. Bloom has isolated nine sub-categories of Knowledge under three headings:

Knowledge of Specifics (1.1) that asks for the recall of simple, concrete elements.

Knowledge of Ways and Means of Dealing with Specifics (1.2) that asks for the recall of knowledge about relationships.

Knowledge of Universals and Abstractions in a Field (1.3) that asks for the recall of complex generalizations and knowledge structures.

While the taxonomy would be quite useful without the sub-categories, they do serve the following functions:

1. They add to the definition of the major category.

2. They classify objectives that might lend themselves to a particular instructional or evaluational approach.

3. They provide for a series of suggestions that one may review in attempting to identify the component objectives of an Objective complex.

4. They provide a series of foci for educational research in exploring each of the major categories.

A definition of each of the nine sub-categories of Knowledge appears below. The skills needed to perform the tasks defined by this book include classifying objectives precisely according to major categories. Precise classification into sub-categories is not required.

1.11 Knowledge of Terminology. Objectives related to the recall of knowledge of the referents for specific symbols or the recall of symbols for specific referents.

1.12 Knowledge of Specific Facts. Objectives related to the recall of knowledge of dates, events, persons, places, etc.

1.21 Knowledge of Conventions. Objectives related to the recall of knowledge of usages, styles, practices and forms that are agreed upon within a field.

1.22 Knowledge of Trends and Sequences. Objectives related to the recall of knowledge of processes, directions and movements of phenomena with respect to time.

1.23 Knowledge of Classifications and Categories. Objectives related to the recall of knowledge of the classes, sets, divisions and arrangements that are basic for a given subject field.

1.24 Knowledge of Criteria. Objectives related to the recall of knowledge of the rule or test by which facts, principles, opinions and conduct are tested or judged.

1.25 Knowledge of Methodology. Objectives related to the recall of knowledge of the method of inquiry, technique, and procedures employed in a particular field as well as those employed in investigating particular problems and phenomena.

1.31 Knowledge of Principles and Generalizations. Objectives related to the recall of knowledge of particular abstractions that summarize observations of phenomena.

1.32 Knowledge of Theories and Structures. Objectives related to the recall of knowledge of the body of principles and generalizations that are interrelated to form a theory or structure.

2.0 COMPREHENSION (Degree to which one should be able to manipulate meaningfully Knowledge elements)	The learner will give evidence of comprehension through: 2.1 Translation 2.2 Interpretation 2.3 Extrapolation

COMPREHENSION (2.0) OBJECTIVE CELLS

A comprehension objective spells out the degree to which a recallable knowledge element should be meaningfully manipulated. For knowledge to be useful in problem-solving or communication, it must be comprehended by the learner. The level of comprehension, however, varies according to how one applies it. Three sub-categories of Comprehension are:

Translation: Part-for-part rephrasing of a communication or restating of a problem.

Interpretation: Summarizing a simple communication or problem situation by reordering or rearranging the original.

Extrapolation: Extending given data to determine implications, consequences, corollaries, etc.

The definitions of the Interpretation and Extrapolation cells tend to overlap with cells in the Synthesis (5.0) category. Bloom recommends that, when in doubt, give the objective the simpler classification. In our modified taxonomy the criterion is based on whether or not the objective is complex-oriented. If it focuses upon an essential component in an objective complex, it should be classified as Analysis, Synthesis, or Evaluation. If not, classify it as Comprehension.

The reader should refer to Foldout II as he reads this chapter, for he will find there an example of each of the objectives taken from a unit on "Critical Listening."

3.0 APPLICATION (Development of complex functional behaviors)	The learner will perform complex tasks in Application situations.

APPLICATION (3.0) OBJECTIVE CELL

Application identifies objectives concerned with the uses to which symbolized knowledge can be put. Since the problem and communication situations under Application could be either theoretical in nature, simulated, imaginary, or real-life, the term "application" should not be considered to be synonymous with "utilitarian." To be correctly classified at this level, an objective should require that more than one knowledge-level objective be manipulated in the production of the responses.

While the author was tempted to divide Application into three sub-categories, this procedure would have made the cells different from Bloom's and would create a problem in communication. To broaden the perspective of the reader, however, a discussion of these categories follows.

There are three general ways in which knowledge is applied by an individual as he manipulates his external and internal world to serve his needs. First, in problem-solving when he is thwarted from reaching his goals by external barriers, his task is to restructure the situation and alter his course of action. Second, in communicating when his spontaneous, intuitive utterances or interpretations fail him, his task again is one of restructuring. The third application is in the self-actualizing process[5] when he is struggling to realize his potential and enhance his self-picture. In this case he is operating in an internal world, and his problems are unique to him. Again, however, his task is one of restructuring.

[5]Self-actualization is a psychological term used by both Kurt Goldstein and A. H. Maslow, referring to the drive in man that makes him persevere to actualize or realize his potentialities — a goal he must reach to maintain or restore his equilibrium.

If sub-categories were provided for Application, they might be:

3.0 APPLICATION

3.1 Problem Solving

3.11 Mechanical: Involves the routine solving of problems through direct application of knowledge.

3.12 Creative: Involves the task of applying higher level skills of the taxonomy (4.0-6.2) in solving problems.

3.2 Communicating

3.21 Mechanical: Involves the routine receiving and transmitting of complex communications through direct application of knowledge.

3.22 Creative: Involves the task of applying higher level skills of the taxonomy (4.0-6.2) in receiving and transmitting complex communications.

3.3 Self-actualizing

3.31 Mechanical: Involves the routine solving of ego-related problems through the direct application of knowledge.

3.32 Creative: Involves the task of applying higher level skills of the taxonomy in solving ego-related problems.

In this book nearly all objectives are derived from the Application (3.0) cell. The preceding analysis may be helpful to the reader in dealing with this category. Some readers may reject the self-actualizing cell, but it is not crucial to the framework.

4.0 ANALYSIS (Development of ability to identify relevant knowledge components in Application situations)	The learner will identify: 4.1 Elements 4.2 Relationships 4.3 Organizational principles relevant to specified application behavior.

ANALYSIS (4.0) OBJECTIVE CELLS

Analysis classifies objectives that are concerned with the identification, in an Application situation, of Knowledge components relevant to the structuring of an adequate performance. The following definitions describe the content of the cells:

4.1 Analysis of Elements. Objectives related to the identification of relevant elements in an Application task situation that are needed for the performance of the task.

4.2 Analysis of Relationships. Objectives related to the identification of relevant relationships that are needed for the performance of an Application task.

4.3 Analysis of Organizational Principles. Objectives related to the identification of structural patterns in an Application task situation that are needed for the performance of the task.

When a learner cannot immediately perceive relationships and respond adequately to an Application task, he needs to analyze the situation. The performer must examine the task to find the components he needs to make a satisfactory response. The learner attempts to match his previous knowledge with the elements in the new situation. In a highly complex task it is likely that both Synthesis and Evaluation skills will also be needed.

5.0 SYNTHESIS (Development of abilities to combine knowledge elements fabricating appropriate Application behaviors)	The learner will combine appropriate knowledge elements into the: 5.1 Production of a Unique Communication 5.2 Production of a Plan or Proposed Set of Operations 5.3 Derivation of a Set of Abstract Relations

SYNTHESIS (5.0) OBJECTIVE CELLS

Synthesis classifies objectives that are concerned with the learner's production of a unique response to an Application task — that is, unique to him. His response would be based upon his synthesis of responses from one or more of the sub-categories below:

5.1 Production of a Unique Communication. Objectives related to the development of a communication in which the writer or speaker attempts to convey ideas or feelings to others.

5.2 Production of a Plan or Proposed Set of Operations. Objectives related to the development of a plan or proposal.

5.3 Derivation of a Set of Abstract Relations. Objectives that require the combining of abstract elements into a new product.

The individual must combine the elements according to his relevant knowledge so that he can produce the appropriate product demanded by the Application task—but the response must have unique characteristics. The response can satisfy this objective once only. If the desired response is to be routine, the objective is classified at the Application level.

6.0 EVALUATION (Development of abilities to appraise the appropriateness of a proposed or applied Application behavior)	The learner will appraise a communication or problem solution with: 6.1 Judgments in terms of Internal Evidence 6.2 Judgments in terms of External Criteria

EVALUATION (6.0) OBJECTIVE CELLS

Evaluation classifies objectives that are concerned with the learner's ability to appraise the adequacy of a synthesis produced either by himself or another. The product to be appraised might be either the solution to a problem or a communication.

The sub-categories of Evaluation are:

6.1 Judgments in terms of Internal Evidence. Objectives related to the appraisal of a product from such evidence as logical accuracy, consistency, and other internal criteria.

6.2 Judgment in terms of External Criteria. Evaluation objectives related to the appraisal of a product with reference to selected or remembered criteria.

While the categories in the classification system identify concepts familiar to most adults, the taxonomy structure refines meanings. In other words, although the language of the taxonomy structure is more attuned to the culture of the society than to educational psychology and philosophy, both the layman and the educator can, with a minimum of effort, learn to communicate within the discipline of the taxonomy.

The language of the classification system seems justified to the author because:

1. Cognitive skills and abilities are dependent upon the individual's competence in using words and symbols to manipulate elements of his past experiences.

2. Cognitive skills and abilities are essential to modern man in three areas: problem solving, communicating and self-actualizing (Application).

3. One cannot solve complex problems or communicate complex ideas without the ability to recall and comprehend meaningful elements of one's past experience (Knowledge and Comprehension).

4. When one attempts to solve a problem or communicate an idea, one must identify the relevant elements and their relationship to each other through *analysis*.

5. When one attempts to *synthesize* a communication or the solution to a problem, one symbolically manipulates the analyzed elements until a plausible course of action is indicated.

6. One then *evaluates* the plausible course of action by trying it overtly, or by appraising it symbolically on the basis of internal consistency or with external criteria.

In the succeeding chapters, the categories will be called "levels."

The Classification System as a Taxonomy

Let us now attempt to appraise this modified taxonomy in terms of the five criteria given on page 4. (The reader is advised to bookmark the capsuled version of the modified taxonomy, page 29, and to refer to the page frequently.) As the modified taxonomy categories are not appreciably different from those of Bloom, this evaluation has relied heavily upon a selected and annotated bibliography by Richard Cox (1966) of the University of Pittsburgh, and John Gordon of the University of Hawaii, entitled, "Validation and Uses of the *Taxonomy of Educational Objectives: Cognitive Domain.*" The compilers of this bibliography play a semi-official role as "keepers of the records" and plan to keep an up-to-date file of the research related to the in-progress and completed research on the cognitive domain. In a symposium at the American Educational Research Association conference in 1966, Cox delivered a paper entitled, "The First Decade," in which he summarized the achievements of the taxonomy to that date. We shall also refer to this paper.

Criterion I — Can the Classification Be Clearly Differentiated?

Research indicates that examination questions and statements of objectives can be classified within the confines of the taxonomy, by independent raters, with a high degree of agreement. Such research is reported in the handbook, and in more recent studies by Stanley and Bolton (1957), McGuire (1963), Stoker and Kropp (1964), and Louise Tyler (1966). Factor analysis studies by Milholland and Zinn (1966), however, indicate that the taxonomy categories are not functionally independent. They point out, rather that the student's general ability, specific interests, and motivation toward grades appear to be the determining factors in his achievement of objectives. Implied here, then, is the notion that the categories are not mutually exclusive of one another.

Criterion II — Is the Taxonomy Comprehensive Enough to Provide Educators and Researchers with All the Categories They Need to Develop Curricula and Construct Adequate Examinations?

All of the studies reported under Criterion I indicate that the taxonomy is comprehensive, to the extent that practically all of the questions which appear on examinations from the elementary through the professional school can be fairly readily classified into the system. Other researchers — Wood (1960), Louise Tyler (1965), and Svitavsky (1966) — have focused upon avowed objectives within existing courses of study, and have found that they can be readily classified. With this evidence, it can be inferred that the taxonomy is comprehensive enough to incorporate nearly all of the current cognitive focal points being used in today's schools.

Criterion III — Are the Categories Compatible with the Existing Language of the Educational Discipline?

If a taxonomy gives narrow, specific meaning to common general terms within the discipline, it fre-

quently creates a barrier to communications, making an elite out of the initiated. This is somewhat of a problem with the Bloom taxonomy, as evidenced in the following paragraph from *Handbook I*:

> Our attempt to arrange educational behaviors from simple to complex was based on the idea that a particular simple behavior may become integrated with other equally simple behaviors to form a more complex behavior. Thus our classifications may be said to be in the form where behaviors of type A form one class, behaviors of type AB form another class, while behaviors of type ABC form still another class. (p. 18).

The Bloom taxonomy structure forces us to think of the major classifications of objectives as a hierarchy, beginning with the simplest — Knowledge — and moving upward through Comprehension, Application, Analysis, and Synthesis, to Evaluation. This implies that Synthesis and Evaluation can apply to complex behaviors, and that what the layman called synthesis must now be attributed to a subheading under Comprehension.

In the Drumheller modified structure the problem has been somewhat reduced by emphasizing the logical relationship between the categories and eliminating the hierarchical emphasis. With this change the layman is again able to understand the meaning of educational statements made using taxonomy definitions.

Criterion IV — Is There a Real Order Among the Phenomena Represented by the Terms?

With reference to the Bloom taxonomy, the answer to this is a qualified "yes." Research by Ayers (1966) and Stoker (1964) provides statistical evidence for the hierarchical structure of the taxonomy. In other words, learnings on the lower levels of the taxonomy tend to be prerequisite to the mastering of objectives on the higher levels. The authors of *Taxonomy of Educational Objectives* (Bloom *et al.,* 1956) clearly state that

> taxonomies . . . have certain structural rules which exceed in complexity the rules of a classification system. While a classification scheme may have many arbitrary elements, a taxonomy scheme may not. A taxonomy must be so constructed that the order of the terms must correspond to some "real" order among the phenomena represented by the terms . . . A taxonomy must be validated by demonstrating its consistency with the theoretical views

in research findings of the field it attempts to order. (p. 17)

If Bloom is resting his case for calling his classification system a taxonomy on its hierarchical structure, his position is quite tenuous.

It might be, however, that in the behavioral sciences we can justify the "taxonomy" concept, not as the other half of a classification dichotomy, but simply as more structured than a classification system. Bloom's system appears to belong in the taxonomy camp, but its theoretical structure is still a little weak. The modified taxonomy, however, emphasizes a stronger structural relationship between the parts which has proven useful in both behavioral analysis and, as we shall see in Chapter V, in curriculum design.

Criterion V—Does the Structure of the Taxonomy Make a Significant Contribution to the Education Discipline Which Is Above and Beyond the Categories Defined?

The following are four major achievements made possible by the applied Bloom taxonomy:

1. It provides a test designer with a general framework, a series of category reminders, and a series of simple examination questions which help to insure the construction of comprehensive examinations. This was a major focus of the designers of the taxonomy, and its value here has been clearly established.
2. It provides a yardstick by which the classroom teacher (or an administrator) can appraise the comprehensiveness of his teaching objectives and examinations (Lawrence, (1963; Scannel and Stellwagen, 1960; Lessinger, 1963).
3. It provides a language which makes it possible to construct objective oriented test questions (Krathwohl, 1965; Stevens, 1965) and to test question banks (Lessinger, 1963), to make the classroom test-construction process more efficient and effective.
4. It provides guidelines for the construction of an instrument for evaluating the relative effectiveness of two or more educational approaches (Tyler, 1966).

It seems readily apparent that the Bloom *Taxonomy of Educational Objectives: Handbook I, Cognitive Domain* has clearly fulfilled a genuine and long-felt need for a systematic approach to the classifying of educational objectives, and the testing for such objectives. It could be, however, that Bloom's entire *Handbook* (hereafter referred to as *Handbook I*), rather than the taxonomy by itself, is the key to its success.

The modified taxonomy with its structural changes continues to serve the above functions while adding the following:

5. It provides a structure which guides the curriculum designer in breaking complex behavioral objectives into teachable components.
6. It provides a structure which enables the designer to sequence component objectives in building complex behaviors.

Using the Taxonomy in Analyzing Behavior

At this point the author asks three questions:

1. Are the taxonomy categories comprehensive enough to classify all the cognitive objectives appropriate for a unit of instruction?
2. Does the taxonomy provide a rationale for illustrating the relationships existing between the various objectives within a unit?
3. Can the taxonomy provide a tool to help in identifying the objectives relevant to a unit?

Before trying to answer these questions, the reader is asked to refer once more to Foldout II in Appendix II, which provides sample objectives from a unit of instruction in critical listening, including samples from all the taxonomy categories. At the left are listed three objectives that provide the focus and purpose for the unit. In the taxonomy being outlined here, the "terminal behavior complexes" are identical to the application objectives in Bloom's taxonomy. All the other objectives can be derived from the application level objectives through *behavior analysis*.

The first step in the process of behavior analysis (see large numeral 1 on Foldout II) is to determine the terminal behavior complexes which legitimately belong in a unit of instruction. In this particular case there are three rather broad objectives which identify the skills needed for critical listening.

The second step is to determine the objectives related to recallable knowledge (Level I of the taxonomy). As described earlier, knowledge is divided into nine cells in a continuum from the concrete-specific on the left to the abstract-general on the right. The central portion of the continuum focuses on Knowledge of Ways and Means of Dealing with Specifics. In selecting appropriate Knowledge objectives, there is one essential criterion: Their mastery should equip the learner with either essential, or very useful, tools for reaching the terminal behavior complex.

Every learner, however, has a different background of experiences and a unique collection of cognitive styles and requires an individual body of knowledge to reach a set of terminal behaviors. It is necessary, then, that the behavior analyst think of the many probable styles and backgrounds of the target population that will use the program. He will then judge on the basis of probability the knowledge elements that should be included. Since this is a difficult task, it is likely that he will make judgmental errors. He will want to consult curriculum experts and compare his work with that of others. Once the curriculum is in use, educators should observe it and conduct field tests to determine its effectiveness. The behavior analyst determines which knowledge components should be included through a logical thought process. Learners, however, will acquire knowledge with different levels of success according to their own abilities.

The third step in the analysis of behavior is to identify the behaviors related to Level IV, Analysis, that are either essential or very helpful in reaching the terminal behaviors. The three cells at this level, as at the Knowledge level, range from the specific-concrete, Analysis of Elements, to the general-abstract, Analysis of Organizational Principles. The major concern of the objectives in this category is that the learner develop the ability to identify relevant knowledge in problems similar to those defined by the terminal objectives. The task of the behavior analyst is to identify the conditions under which the learner is expected to pick out the knowledge-related components in a problem situation or a communication. Note that this enables the analyst to build all the "need to know" comprehensions into his analysis, synthesis

and evaluation objectives. This means that the comprehension objectives are attached last and are restricted to "nice to know."

The fourth step in the analysis of behavior is concerned with Level V, Synthesis, and two questions: Under what circumstances might the learner be required to synthesize a discipline-related response, and what are the behaviors necessary to fabricate the responses? The analysis of terminal behaviors at the Analysis, Synthesis, and Evaluation Levels might direct one toward a considerable number of knowledge components (especially in the "Ways and Means of Dealing with Specifics" level), which would be added to those uncovered in the second step. The three cells in Level V advance in order of degree of abstraction.

In this structure, Levels IV-VI have been subordinated to Level III, Application. The rationale for this is that, in practice they are called upon when needed in the Application process, and it is quite conceivable that they might never be needed. In the area of critical listening, for example, an individual may have an instinctive ability to penetrate quickly the veneer of a speaker to identify his real motives. The process may seem to be an unconscious one, and such an individual may not know how he made his appraisal. Such a learner seems to need little training in analysis in this area, while another might need much training. The first learner, however, may need some evaluation skills to help him when his intuition fails. This taxonomy structure clearly identifies a research area that needs exploration: To what extent is training in analysis, synthesis, and evaluation necessary or even useful to the learner who can perform terminal behaviors without them? The author's assumption is that a student cannot depend on intuition so that he should master the necessary skills to help him when intuition fails.

Level VI, Evaluation, is the emphasis of the fifth step in the analysis of behavior. How can one identify the behaviors needed to either defend an appraisal of a communication or defend an appraisal of a solution to a problem? The first of the two cells in Level VI focuses on the internal consistency of the product being appraised, while the second focuses on the external validity of the product.

The sixth step is to determine the degree to which an individual can comprehend or manipulate the "nice to know" elements of recalled knowledge as well as the understandings needed to allow for minor differences in the cognitive styles of the learners. This is a concern for Level II, Comprehension. The guidelines that determine the degree of comprehension needed are again derived from terminal behaviors. At this point the analyst must ascertain at which of three levels the learner stands. A rather profound understanding of the knowledge referents may be needed by the learner so that he can "extrapolate" beyond his data. Possibly, however, he would be adequately prepared if he could simply "interpret" the relevance of a knowledge element to a situation. Or again, perhaps all that would be necessary would be for the learner to "translate" or rephrase the knowledge-oriented statement so that it becomes clear to him. In practice, if the comprehension skills are defined at Levels III-VI of the taxonomy, they are not spelled out at Level II. This procedure streamlines the design process without creating any difficulties.

To return now to the questions asked on page 23:

1. Yes, the modified taxonomy is comprehensive enough to classify all the cognitive objectives appropriate for a unit of instruction. Research indicates that when the taxonomy is used to classify test items or objectives that were structured without its aid, the taxonomy is equal to the task. The preceding discussion additionally shows how an apparently comprehensive set of objectives emerges from the taxonomy when one focuses on the desired terminal objectives.

2. The preceding discussion has pointed out that the Knowledge and Comprehension objectives define the raw materials. The Analysis, Synthesis and Evaluation, on the other hand, define the high order of instrumental behaviors needed to accomplish the long-range terminal behaviors — the Application objectives. This rationale provides the glue for claiming this as a taxonomy, and for showing the interrelationship each cell has with every other cell.

3. The greatest strength and use of the taxonomy is in helping to identify the objectives relevant to a unit. If one can identify from one to five or six terminal behaviors that would incorporate all, or nearly all, the concerns of a unit, the taxonomy can

provide a blueprint for determining the intermediate objectives as described in the step-by-step procedure. The analyst, before he can be satisfied that his list of objectives is adequate, would systematically explore each cell of the taxonomy. By doing so, he could then identify any key concepts or skills that had not been thus far identified.

A Limitation of the Terminal Behavior Focus

The general application of this modified taxonomy to the curriculum of the public school is dependent upon the answer to the question, "Is there a reasonable number of definable terminal behavior complexes that would provide the teacher with a focus for most of his educational concerns?" It is possible that a teacher might have to use another orientation if the taxonomy approach were not applicable to a subject matter discipline or if one were needed to refine the curriculum. Generally, however, if the modified taxonomy is used, it should provide the basis for curriculum design.

Exploring the sometimes-overlapping dichotomy between things that are "nice to know" and those that one "needs to know" may provide the necessary insights into the question raised above. Let us examine a "needs to know" element within the framework of Robert Havighurst's developmental task (1953):

> A task which arises at or about a certain period in the life of the individual, successful achievement of which leads to his happiness and to success with later tasks, while failure leads to unhappiness in the individual, disapproval by the society, and difficulty with later tasks.

Walking and talking are developmental tasks for all normal children, while the ability to perform an appendectomy is a task for the student of surgery. If one needs to know something, it must have a function; and it must, therefore, be classified as a developmental task.

On the other hand, many "nice to know" elements are included in the curriculum because they are intrinsically interesting to students and motivate them or because the instructor or the society thinks they are nice to know.

Such elements may be part of a long-range set of terminal behaviors in which case they would invariably be identified when the terminal complex is plugged into the taxonomy mill. Or they might be isolated comprehensions that would not be discovered through a task analysis.

Although these isolated, nice-to-know understandings are not crucial to many disciplines, they are often included in texts and classroom discussions and are more an element of methodology than of curriculum design.

One common academic discipline — world history — seems to have objectives that could be classified almost totally as "nice to know." The subject does not consist of adolescent developmental tasks (except for future social studies teachers) and there is so little future reinforcement of the concepts presented that they are soon forgotten. Sometimes the course is organized around such terminal behavior complexes as: "The Government Under Pericles," "The Protestant Reformation," etc. It is possible to analyze these complexes and to organize a self-contained unit of instruction. The expected behaviors are concerned with the learner's ability to communicate his comprehension as he responds to questions about the complex. When one examines the elements actually taught in most world history courses, however, one finds that most elements are not part of complexes but are isolated "nice to know" comprehensions. In such courses, where tradition dictates the content, the taxonomy-centered analysis approach to the identification of objectives is not feasible unless

new terminal behaviors are defined which focus upon applications of learnings, such as: The learner will explain, using historical referents, the arguments for and against "civil disobedience" in a contemporary situation.

In instruction that is oriented toward developmental tasks, however, the modified taxonomy serves as the major device for identifying objectives.

The writer is convinced that the needs-to-know tasks of education are finite and, in many areas, number ten or less. For example, Foldout II of Appendix II contains a set of essential critical listening terminal objectives. A list four or five times as long could contain *all* terminal listening objective complexes. Communication skills are a composite of writing, speaking, reading, and listening skills. Extend that same list a few times for a rough estimate of the length of a list of communication terminal objectives. Prerequisite behavior objectives can then be derived through a logical analysis of the terminal objectives, verified through controlled field testing.

Students will continue to need to be motivated and to be conversant with subjects that are part of the culture so that the authors of curriculum materials will continue to make materials interesting by including much of the "nice to know." The "needs to know" objectives within the discipline defined here, however, provide the specifications for writing effective curriculum materials and for teaching the course, and such objectives are of primary importance.

Structure of a Modified Taxonomy of Educational Objectives*

MAJOR CATEGORIES	SUB-CATEGORIES		
1.0 KNOWLEDGE: (Development of ability to recall appropriate information, with or without comprehension)	The learner will verbally recall:		
	KNOWLEDGE OF SPECIFICS	KNOWLEDGE OF WAYS & MEANS OF DEALING WITH SPECIFICS	KNOWLEDGE OF UNIVERSALS & ABSTRACTIONS IN A FIELD
	1.11 Knowledge of terms 1.12 Knowledge of specific facts	1.21 Knowledge of conventions 1.22 Knowledge of trends & sequences 1.23 Knowledge of classifications & categories 1.24 Knowledge of criteria 1.25 Knowledge of methodology	1.31 Knowledge of principles & generalizations 1.32 Knowledge of theories and structures
2.0 COMPREHENSION: (Degree to which one should be able to manipulate meaningfully Knowledge elements)	The learner will give evidence of comprehension through: 2.1 Translation 2.2 Interpretation 2.3 Extrapolation beyond data		
3.0 APPLICATION: (Development of complex functional behaviors)	The learner will perform complex tasks in Application situations.		
4.0 ANALYSIS: (Development of ability to identify relevant knowledge components in Application situations)	The learner will identify: 4.1 Elements 4.2 Relationships 4.3 Organizational principles relevant to specified application behavior		
5.0 SYNTHESIS: (Development of ability to combine knowledge elements in fabricating appropriate Application behaviors)	The learner will combine appropriate knowledge elements into the: 5.1 Production of a unique communication 5.2 Production of a plan or proposed set of operations 5.3 Derivation of a set of abstract relations		
6.0 EVALUATION: (Development of ability to appraise the appropriateness of a proposed or applied Application behavior)	The learner will appraise a communication or problem solution with: 6.1 Judgments in terms of internal evidence 6.2 Judgments in terms of external criteria		

*See page 17.

IV
A Model for Curriculum Design

Now that the format has been established, a rationale given for the behaviorally-oriented objective, and an analysis made of how to turn terminal behavior complexes into teachable sub-objectives, this chapter will introduce a model for organizing objectives into a pattern. The resulting pattern will be specific enough to serve as a blueprint for designing a curriculum and for writing any supplementary materials.

The author considers the following four characteristics of the Drumheller model to be essential for defining an orientation to curriculum design. The model provides:

1. A format and the criteria for adapting a comprehensive set of objective complexes to a unit of instruction.

2. A format and the criteria that define the degrees of freedom of the writer or the teacher in developing curricula.

3. A format that is compatible with contemporary learning theory and educational practice.

4. A format that eliminates the need for restating the same objectives over and over again.

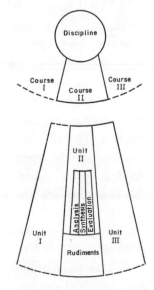

The model appears in two forms — a basic version developed on the following pages and a self-explanatory overview in Foldout III in Appendix II.

The diagram directly above shows the organizational structure of an educational discipline. The term "discipline" is used to mean the integral collection of related behavior complexes of a field of specialization. These complexes, when mastered, give one a functional competence in dealing with Application tasks related to the field. For example, mathematics, cherry picking, ancient history, dishwashing, and baseball pitching could be considered disciplines under this definition.

Disciplines differ in complexity and in the amount of time required for learners to master them. Dishwashing can be mastered in a few hours or less, while mathematics mastery may take years. Complex disciplines, therefore, require sub-divisions both for ordering the discipline's objective foci and for presenting it systematically to the learner. The "unit" is the key sub-division in this design model. For instructional purposes, a discipline is divided into, and presented in, one or more sequenced units.

The portion of the diagram enclosed by a heavy black line provides the basic structure of the design model and has a unit focus. If the discipline of mathematics were divided into units according to the diagram, there would be scores of spokes in the wheel.

The term "modular" is used to indicate that these units are truly specific, essential blocks that are integral parts of an overall developmental design. Also implied is the notion that a unit built to identical specifications can replace an original block without loss. This means that a basic curriculum may be varied to include alternate units geared to the interests and cognitive styles of the learner that could be substituted for the original, yet lead to the same objectives. The design model lends itself to a modular approach to curriculum development.

Objective-Oriented Curriculum Subdivisions

Many curriculum designers and teachers, when formulating instructional objectives, find themselves stating and restating objectives — at the course level, the unit level, the sub-unit level, and the lesson level. The process is exhausting, yet it seems to be necessary. And, all too frequently, this difficulty results in one's settling for something short of a systematic approach to stating objectives. To overcome the problem of repeating objectives, this book presents, in a design model, a scheme for subdividing and organizing the curriculum. It utilizes five classifications: The sequence level, the course level, the unit level, the sub-unit level, and the rudimentary level. Taxonomy categories have been assigned to each of the sequence sub-divisions. Whereas the cognitive objectives, down to and including the unit level, are application centered, the objectives of the sub-units emphasize analysis, synthesis, and evaluation. Objectives at the rudimentary level are primarily knowledge-centered.

This procedure makes it necessary to distinguish between the terms "sequence objectives" and "sequence-level objectives"; "unit objectives" and "unit-level objectives"; etc. When objectives are specified in this way, they need not be repeated at the various levels. In addition, one can see at a glance all the objectives relevant to a sub-unit objective. In other words, once the terminal objectives have been set in terms of the design model, there is little need for rewriting them for each lesson. (The reader may look at Foldout IV in Appendix II to get a preview of a format for stating objectives within the framework of the model). The sequenced sub-units then provide the structure for the development of the unit terminal behavior complexes. This focus insures that objectives from all levels of the taxonomy will get an adequate emphasis.

Before proceeding to read about the cells in the model, the reader is asked to remember that, except for the introductory sub-unit, only terminal behavior objectives are spelled out in this design. Transitional objectives are left to the writer or teacher to specify and pursue. Since nearly all the transitional objectives of learning are concerned with methodology or means rather than ends, the teacher or writer must interject transitional objectives that serve a temporary function in the educational process. This is his domain.

Structure of the Drumheller Design Model

The model described in this chapter serves as a blueprint for designing, or guiding, learning activities in a curriculum unit, based upon objectives determined through the use of the modified taxonomy. It defines an organizational scheme for sequencing and reinforcing learning experiences so that one can always see the relationship of the part to the whole. Much freedom, however, is left to the writer or teacher in that he can specify the particular experiences, the motivation and rewards systems, the role of the teacher, the groupings of students, etc.

Application Objectives (Objective Complexes)

The design model portrays a blending of a conventional unit format and the modified taxonomy headings. Each cell is given a label identifying it in both frameworks. The long-range sequence and course objectives are stated in terms of terminal behavior complexes that can be divided and subdivided into component complexes until the unit level is reached. The unit-level objectives then become the simplest of the complexes. And these are further divided by the behavior analysis process to produce the objectives for the remainder of the cells of the model.

Rudimentary Objectives

The rudimentary terminal behavior objectives are concerned primarily with knowledge and provide the foundation upon which higher curriculum levels (and behavior levels) are built. Essential tools in the whole curriculum structure, they are easily identified, translated, interpreted, etc. Therefore, the learner should have the opportunity to respond to them in situations where his responses can be evaluated and correct ones reinforced. The general pattern of reinforcement fits into a Skinnerian scheme of scheduling, but an added dimension is present. The sub-unit concerns for the higher level objectives of the taxonomy define the context in which the student is to identify the rudiment and respond to it.

Referring to the model (see Foldout III in Appendix II), one can see that as the individual proceeds through sub-units, he first identifies the knowledge elements in analysis situations (see arrow). He then uses knowledge elements to create syntheses (see arrow). In Sub-Unit IV, as he evaluates, he is constantly interacting with the knowledge elements. Finally, he uses the knowledge in both simulated and real experiences in Sub-Unit V in polishing the terminal performances. A symbolic illustration of the scheduled performances of "Knowledge" tasks is indicated by the "I" (for initial) and the "R" (for reinforcement).

The student usually gets his first exposures to the rudiment in a context focused upon the unit objective complexes. For this reason, comprehension objectives need not be specified for terminal behavior sub-objectives. The built-in scheduling procedure actually defines the comprehension requirements for the rudimentary Knowledge objectives.

Sub-Unit Objectives

The sub-unit terminal behavior objectives are complex — Analysis-, Synthesis-, and Evaluation-oriented. Looking at the chart, one sees that five sub-unit cells have been identified in terms of a gestalt-based learning framework. These sub-units could be subdivided or combined so that a unit may have from two to ten or more sub-units. But the sub-unit educational functions described in the model would still have to be carefully reassigned in the new format. In some units the teacher might take only a few minutes to present Sub-Unit I adequately, while he might take several weeks to present Sub-Unit II. In another unit, the converse might be true. The model assures that all the terminal sub-objectives will be attended to.

Sub-Units I and V are more method-oriented than the others, and these components will be discussed in detail in Chapter V. The major concern of Sub-Unit I is a transitional one: to elicit responses from the student—responses that indicate the student comprehends the nature of the terminal behavior complexes of the unit to the extent that he can describe them and be motivated to participate in learning activities that enable him to acquire them.

As the learner tries to define the terminal complexes, he will probably recognize some essential terminal sub-objectives that he has already achieved and some that he needs. The student is not expected to reach any of the terminal sub-objectives in Sub-Unit I. He will, however, be expected to reach a group of terminal sub-objectives in each of the other sub-units.

The sub-unit objectives are cumulative; that is, when Sub-Unit II is begun, its objectives are central, but the objectives of Sub-Unit I are still important. During Sub-Unit IV three sets of behaviors from previous sub-units still need to be included for reinforcement. The research indicating the hierarchical quality of Bloom's taxonomy is reassuring because it implies that a focus on higher level objectives tends to provide an automatic reinforcement of the lower-level behaviors.

Sub-Unit V has the unit complexes as its focus and is directed toward polishing the student's performance until he demonstrates the terminal behaviors. It is the only sub-unit that has mastery of the behavior complex as a major emphasis. Any student who can perform at this level of proficiency early in the unit has completed the unit. Typically, instruction units do not demand a functional competency in the performance of complex behaviors. Sub-Unit V, on the other hand, requires such performance and insures that the writer or teacher will provide time and experiences to enable its acquisition.

Sub-Unit II focuses on the Analysis objectives of the modified taxonomy and seeks to help the student interpret all the rudimentary elements in terms of analysis. This model furnishes the teacher and writer with a map defining all the terminal objectives of which he should be aware at any moment in the unit, from the sequence to the rudimentary level. Some Knowledge objectives are more appropriate to some sub-units than to others. For example, Classifications and Categories may be more appropriate to Analysis; Methodology may be more appropriate to Synthesis; and Criteria may be more appropriate to Evaluation. When this is the case, there will probably be more reinforcements of these behaviors in one sub-unit than in the others.

Sub-Unit III focuses on Synthesis and is designed to aid the student in interpreting all the rudimentary elements in terms of Synthesis. The interest in Analysis, however, although it is subordinate, is maintained and reinforced. The emphasis of Sub-Unit IV is on Evaluation. It seeks to help the student to interpret all the rudimentary elements in terms of Evaluation. Again Analysis and Synthesis are involved, but they play a subordinate role.

In summary, the sub-unit terminal objective provides the structure for sequencing the learning experiences toward achievement of unit terminal objectives. Teachers and writers should select actual learning experiences on the basis of their effectiveness within the structure.

Cognition Related Affective and Psycho-Motor Objectives

Affective and Psycho-Motor related cognitive objectives appear in two places in the model — near the top, bridging from the course to the unit-level terminal behavior complexes, and in the rudimentary level.

When the Bloom taxonomy was originally conceived, it was considered to be one of three domains — the Cognitive, the Affective, and the Psycho-Motor. Handbooks have been written for the first two, but little has been done with the third. The writer feels that some cognizance should be taken of the motor and the affective (attitudinal) components of cognitive behavior development with respect to the unit terminal behavior complexes. The maxim that "you can lead a horse to water, but you can't make him drink" dramatizes the need for the development of favorable attitudes toward the terminal behaviors of a unit of instruction. When one uses the Design Model, one must specify the attitudes and values to be developed to insure that the terminal behaviors will occur in situations other than a classroom evaluation session. The transitional affective sub-unit objectives will be discussed in Chapter V.

The restrictions of the model allow for consideration of only a small portion of the affective domain, but a portion that is essential in reaching cognitive terminal behavior complexes. The desired response is dependent upon the development of an appropriate attitude. It often takes considerable time to develop an attitude to the point where it is dominant. Therefore, provision has been made at the rudimentary level (see model) for the writer or teacher to attend to the attitude developing task periodically and systematically. Students may need more than one unit to acquire the specified attitude which is the reason for the bridge in the model indicating a course, or sequence, concern.

The Psycho-Motor sub-objectives defined by the Design Model would be "needs to know" and may serve the following functions:

1. The student must perform the psycho-motor task within a specified time.
2. The student must perform the psycho-motor task with a specified degree of dexterity, agility, grace or similar quality.

Taking a simple example from chemistry, one might suppose that one complex of a unit in laboratory skills deals with cleaning and taking care of glassware. A student who keeps his glassware clean but takes two-thirds of every class to do it, breaking much of it and causing considerable expense, is not meeting the psycho-motor requirements of the task even though he rates high in affective and cognitive achievement.

As in the case of the Affective components, the Psycho-Motor objectives may require more than a unit's exposure, and the task may be assigned to a course-level objective.

Additional Values of the Design Model

Within the model proposed in this book the instructional unit is a relatively independent package.

It contains well defined application objectives, has its own motivation and reward structure, and possesses built-in provisions for the achievement of objectives at all levels of the cognitive taxonomy. On the other hand, to the teacher using the unit materials, based on the model, it is simply a good, well organized unit; it remains within the traditional unit format.

The author feels that a motivation and reward system is part of the model because:

1. The unit terminal behaviors can be precisely defined and demonstrated so that the student can identify — and identify *with* — his objectives.

2. The writer and the teacher are committed to the task of eliciting terminal behaviors and are continually directed toward the building-in of response and reward opportunities.

3. Cognitive-related components in the affective domain are specified, to focus attention on the building of favorable attitudes toward the terminal behaviors.

4. With terminal behaviors clearly described, the student can recognize the achievements he is making toward his goal, either with or without built-in appraisal periods.

The model also provides for an emphasis on objectives at all levels of the taxonomy:

1. A major emphasis is placed on the Application objectives, or the terminal behavior complexes, during the first and last sub-unit. This enables the learner to first identify the goal and appraise the status of his achievements, and finally to perform the task until the desired facility is reached.

2. In the second, third, and fourth sub-units, Analysis, Synthesis, and Evaluation are in turn emphasized. Studies of the Bloom taxonomy have shown that even though teachers considered these levels important, teachers had difficulty providing for ample instruction time and evaluation. This format insures that levels 4-6 each get the focus of attention.

3. At the rudimentary objective level, systematic recall and reinforcement of the knowledge, comprehension, psycho-motor, and affective objectives of both this and related units are called for. Although no particular techniques are specified for carrying out these provisions, the writer or the teacher can hardly undertake the task without a sound plan.

That the model defines a unit well within the traditional concept of a unit will be better understood by reading the following excerpts from a U. S. Office of Education publication (Hill, 1963).[6]

The vast explosion of knowledge and man's other space age achievements present a tremendous challenge to . . . teachers . . . to select and organize the learning experiences of children in such a way as to be adequate and effective for living in these times and the years ahead. Unit planning and teaching is one of the best ways to provide for learning experiences on a sufficiently broad base for the requirements of living in today's world.

The unit has been defined as:

An organization of various activities, experiences, and types of learning around a central problem, or purpose, developed cooperatively by a group of pupils under teacher leadership; involves planning, execution of plans, and evaluation of results.

Through unit planning and teaching, the social studies and other learning experiences of the children can be kept up-to-date, vitalized, and brimming with challenge. Such units can be large enough in scope to hold values and interests for every child in a group; they can provide for sufficient depth in study to satisfy the most earnest student.

The unit method is based upon a gestalt or organismic type of psychology, in which figure-field relationships are important. Such relationships mean the relation of one element or item with all of the other elements in its field or area. Insight is a significant element in such learning. The learner explores a new area or unit to discover what it is all about. As he gains information and understanding, insight develops.

Problem solving, research activities, and action characterize much of the pupils' learning efforts in a unit experience. Often direct learning experiences have a major role in the development of the unit, rather than vicarious experiences only . . . the psychological principle of closure is observed as a unit is rounded out and completed, while further goals and achievements are coming into view.

[6]Hill, Wilhelmina. *Unit Planning and Teaching in Elementary Social Studies.* Washington, D.C.: U.S. Dept. of Health, Education, and Welfare, Dept. of Education, 1963, pp. 1-3.

Many teachers are familiar with the unit approach to teaching within the gestalt framework, use the unit, and like it.[7] The structure provided by the Design Model insures that the materials based upon it include a comprehensive set of objectives and systematically emphasize every objective as the behavior complexes are synthesized.

The model, together with the objectives discussed in the next chapter, provides the guidelines needed for a team approach to the development of curricula and curriculum materials.

[7]Another antecedent to current unit-teaching practices was the Herbartian Formal Steps in teaching. This theory of the teaching process was accepted by most educational leaders in the United States throughout the latter half of the nineteenth century. These steps, listed below, are remarkably similar to the emphases in the various sub-units in the design model:

"1. Preparation. An application of the doctrine of interest and apperception, this undertook to put the learner into a receptive mood and mind. The lesson's purpose was explained, and such previous knowledge as might throw light upon the new was mustered into service.

2. Presentation. The new material was set forth and explained.

3. Association. The new material was compared with the old and familiar, and relevant likenesses and differences were noted.

4. Generalization. The several facts developed in the foregoing were framed into a general statement or principle or rule.

5. Application. True to the ancient dictum that nothing is ever learned until it can be readily employed, the learner's understanding of the generalization was put to practice with appropriate problems and exercises."

Meyer, Adolphe E. *An Educational History of the Western World.* New York: McGraw-Hill, 1965, p. 362.

V
Implementing the Design Model

This chapter treats three problems related to implementing the proposed design model:

1. Discriminating between the natures of the designer's objectives (terminal) and the writer's or the teacher's objectives (transitional) in each cell of the model.
2. Developing a "portfolio of objectives" for displaying all the terminal objectives of a unit on a single chart to see their relationships.
3. Efficiently incorporating all the objectives into a linear learning program.

An Instruction Oriented Sub-Model

Transitional objectives have been defined as "method-oriented objectives" that the teacher or the writer identifies as desirable tools for reaching the terminal behaviors by a selected route. For the most part, these objectives have no application after the learner has acquired the terminal behaviors.

Teachers sometimes fail to distinguish between ends and means objectives. The difference is an important one because it distinguishes between the criteria to be used in determining the degree of proficiency expected at the termination of instruction and in appraising irrelevant vestiges of methodological crutches. A concentration of items related to transi-

tional objectives can completely invalidate an examination.[8]

The sub-model (see figure on page 40) in this chapter serves the following functions:

1. It helps the reader make the distinction between a terminal objective and a transitional one.
2. It helps the writer and the teacher identify their responsibilities in pursuing objectives.
3. It identifies one approach to developing curriculum based on the design model, which the writer or the teacher may use or reject. (The value of the design model is in no way dependent upon the acceptance of the sub-model.)

This sub-model corresponds in organization to the sub-unit and rudimentary cell structures of the design model. Where the design model specifies the terminal behavior objectives of the unit, the sub-unit model defines some of the corresponding transitional objectives that may be appropriate.

[8]One argument might be that many of the knowledge and comprehension sub-objectives of the terminal complexes are also transitional. The counter-argument is that when the learner is one day confronted with a problem or communication he cannot decipher, he may need to revert to an academic approach and solve it by the book. This happens to the best golfer, the best administrator, the best teacher, etc. Transitional objectives, however, do not fill this need.

The transitional objectives of the sub-units have been selected because they fit into a somewhat traditional, gestalt-oriented teaching procedure. One using this approach is continually interested in the degree of the student's involvement in comprehending complex-related ideas (closure) and finds it necessary to force the student into periodic appraisal sessions in which the student identifies his accomplishments and tasks yet to be mastered. These are "leveling" and "sharpening" concerns, requiring performance on the part of the student, and are therefore real transitional objectives. The student is also required to respond meaningfully at each sub-unit. Looking again at the sub-model, the reader will note that these transitional objectives are cumulative until the complex has been mastered; the need for them then disappears.

A similar battery of transitional objectives is needed at the rudimentary level. The knowledge components are sterile and uninviting unless they are related to personal experiences and lead to the terminal complexes. Within this gestalt framework, the transitional behavior and the terminal behavior elements form an organic structure through a series of cognitive structures. These structures are developed by concentrating on comprehension of transitional and terminal knowledge elements above the 1.22 level (classifications, criteria, methods, generalizations, and structures). The learner can be kept involved as long as the structures make sense, and he receives reinforcements. Some rudimentary transitional objective concerns that apply to most categories have been noted in the figure on page 40.

This sub-design model is intended more as an indicator of what has been omitted from the master model than as a blueprint for the development of curriculum materials. The distinctions it forces one to make, however, highlight both the limits of the master model and the freedom it gives to the writer and the teacher. The teacher typically spends a large portion of teaching time building up to, and justifying, the terminal behaviors, by concentrating on comprehensions. It is likely, therefore, that most of his transitional objectives can be classified under comprehension.

A Portfolio of Objectives

It has been stated that the design model requires an orderly, concise statement of the terminal objectives of a unit of instruction. In the next few paragraphs, the format of Foldout IV, a Portfolio of Objectives, will be described that will give the teacher and the writer an overview of the terminal objectives of a unit. These objectives will be relevant at any stage of the unit's presentation. The foldout is a reduced-size model of the Portfolio, containing examples from a shoe-tying unit developed in Chapter VI.

Of necessity, the objectives must be condensed in the portfolio. This, however, creates no problems, since the objectives are stated in a complete form as they are developed by the designer. The complete form should accompany the chart form. For the beginner, the design model can be superimposed as it has been on the foldout (see yellow lines).

Each of the cells of the design model has been provided for, and each of the six boxes should be 8½" x 11". Larger sheets may be used in larger units.

A series of columns appears after the entry for each objective. The designer would probably work principally with three columns — "prerequisite objectives," "needs to know," and "total (minimum)." With respect to the prerequisite entry, the designer must inform the writer and the teacher that the student has previously achieved the behavior and needs merely to reinforce it until it again reaches the desired level of proficiency. The writer and the teacher must also know that the student "needs to know" the behavior.

It is the third specification — minimum number of reinforced student responses required — to which many may object. It may imply that the specifications are left to the caprice of the designer, which in turn ties the hands of the writer and forces his material into a mechanical press. It is possible that this might happen if the taxonomy were not hierarchical in structure, and if the model contained many "nice to knows." As it is, however, a performance fulfilling a higher level objective insists that the student perform a series of behaviors called for by lower level objectives. If the knowledge objectives are truly "needs to knows," then much of the needed reinforcement will be a natural consequence of the higher level focus.

Numbers placed in the total column will usually be based upon an editorial policy and will, therefore, tend to be identical — say, 10 or 15. If the designer feels that it is desirable to increase or modify the total occasionally, it is his prerogative. As the writer develops his materials, he can keep a tally on the chart, by sub-units, of the responses demanded. It should be evident then that Sub-Unit II would contain most of the analysis responses, Sub-Unit III the synthesis responses, and so forth. Although the minimum specifications are guidelines, curriculum developers should have the opportunity to deviate from the minimums if they can justify their reason.

A teacher who uses materials based on the design model, especially in individualized instruction, will find the Portfolio, along with its reinforcement schedule, invaluable in guiding the learner and helping him with his problems.

The comprehension section of the Portfolio contains only the isolated terminal comprehensions considered "needs to know." There are many more comprehension objectives, but they are transitional and are selected by the writer or the teacher to implement his methodology. The comprehension objectives have been placed parallel to the unit level because they are, in a sense, miniature isolated complexes. When these isolated terminal comprehensions become too numerous, the design model ceases to serve a useful purpose and might better be discarded.

The unit to which this design model can be applied should focus on a few terminal objective complexes, to which a few isolated terminal comprehension objectives have been appended. This procedure will probably mean that more units will be needed in traditional disciplines to reduce the number of complexes per unit. It will also mean that more complexes will have to be devised to incorporate what are now "nice to know" comprehension "musts." The number of disciplines to which this approach can be applied is not yet known. Mathematics and science clearly are adaptable. History and literature do not fit neatly into the scheme. It is the author's hope that others will find application for the design model in a variety of disciplines.

Linear Programming

The design model leaves one with the impression

that one can easily package a handful of terminal behavioral objective complexes and align the packages to form a course or sequence of instruction. The assumption is that the unit is the smallest curriculum package based on the behavior complex. This is not quite true. It has been mentioned that the teacher can introduce his own "nice to know" complexes into a unit, as well as transitional behavior complexes. In addition to this, the unit objectives might require that several rather complex minor objectives be developed at intervals throughout the unit. For instance, to perform a unit terminal behavior complex, it might be necessary that one recall a theoretical structure such as Darwin's theory of evolution, or Freud's theory of ego defense mechanisms. Or it might be necessary that one recall a method for determining the number of calories in an ounce of cooked corn. These performances might have already been mastered in previous units, or in other sequences, or it might be necessary to develop them in the current unit. Within the framework of the model, these minor complexes are treated as knowledge elements. That is, when the knowledge is needed, a "break" is taken in the development of the unit objectives to develop the ability to recall or identify the elements of the minor complex. This interruption may take from a minute to several hours.

Such a relationship is described in the chart on page 43. Note that in the situation described, the three complexes are so closely related to each other that no differentiation in their treatment occurs until almost two hours have elapsed. During this time, the presentation is interrupted only twice — first, for a session on the development of an ability to recall a structure, and second, to develop an ability to interpret a relationship. Complexes II and III are then developed simultaneously, and Complex I is tabled until the latter part of Sub-Unit III, when it is taken up in isolation. Further interruptions occur as transitional objectives need attention, with methodology as the concern, and when previously developed behaviors need reinforcing.

The chart graphically emphasizes the need for keeping the number of unrelated objective complexes and the number of isolated terminal comprehensions at a minimum.

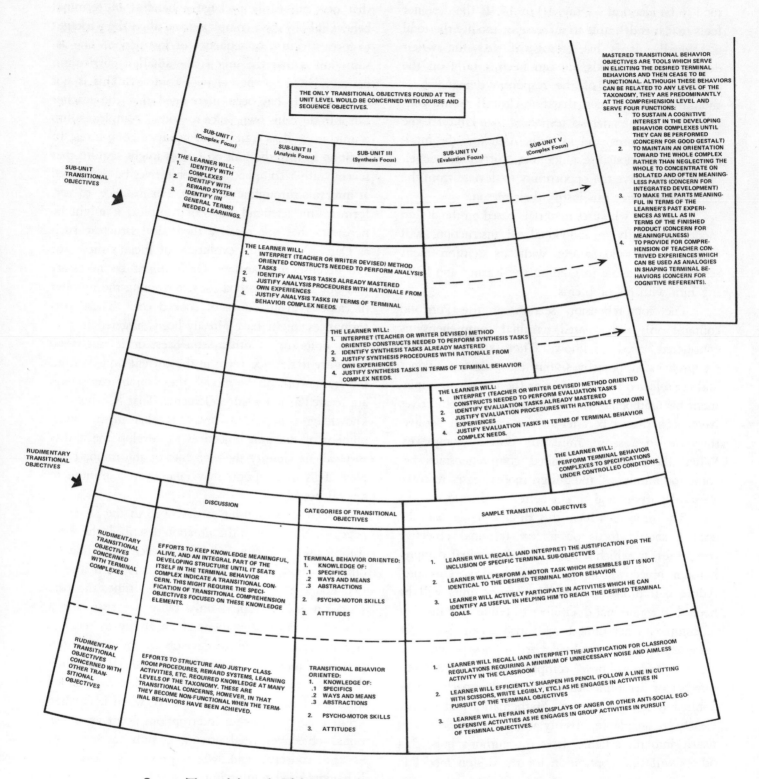

THE ONLY TRANSITIONAL OBJECTIVES FOUND AT THE UNIT LEVEL WOULD BE CONCERNED WITH COURSE AND SEQUENCE OBJECTIVES.

MASTERED TRANSITIONAL BEHAVIOR OBJECTIVES ARE TOOLS WHICH SERVE IN ELICITING THE DESIRED TERMINAL BEHAVIORS AND THEN CEASE TO BE FUNCTIONAL. ALTHOUGH THESE BEHAVIORS CAN BE RELATED TO ANY LEVEL OF THE TAXONOMY, THEY ARE PREDOMINANTLY AT THE COMPREHENSION LEVEL AND SERVE FOUR FUNCTIONS:

1. TO SUSTAIN A COGNITIVE INTEREST IN THE DEVELOPING BEHAVIOR COMPLEXES UNTIL THEY CAN BE PERFORMED (CONCERN FOR GOOD GESTALT)
2. TO MAINTAIN AN ORIENTATION TOWARD THE WHOLE COMPLEX RATHER THAN NEGLECTING THE WHOLE TO CONCENTRATE ON ISOLATED AND OFTEN MEANINGLESS PARTS (CONCERN FOR INTEGRATED DEVELOPMENT)
3. TO MAKE THE PARTS MEANINGFUL IN TERMS OF THE LEARNER'S PAST EXPERIENCES AS WELL AS IN TERMS OF THE FINISHED PRODUCT (CONCERN FOR MEANINGFULNESS)
4. TO PROVIDE FOR COMPREHENSION OF TEACHER CONTRIVED EXPERIENCES WHICH CAN BE USED AS ANALOGIES IN SHAPING TERMINAL BEHAVIORS (CONCERN FOR COGNITIVE REFERENTS).

SUB-UNIT I (Complex Focus)

SUB-UNIT II (Analysis Focus)

SUB-UNIT III (Synthesis Focus)

SUB-UNIT IV (Evaluation Focus)

SUB-UNIT V (Complex Focus)

SUB-UNIT TRANSITIONAL OBJECTIVES

THE LEARNER WILL:
1. IDENTIFY WITH COMPLEXES
2. IDENTIFY WITH REWARD SYSTEM
3. IDENTIFY (IN GENERAL TERMS) NEEDED LEARNINGS.

THE LEARNER WILL:
1. INTERPRET (TEACHER OR WRITER DEVISED) METHOD ORIENTED CONSTRUCTS NEEDED TO PERFORM ANALYSIS TASKS
2. IDENTIFY ANALYSIS TASKS ALREADY MASTERED
3. JUSTIFY ANALYSIS PROCEDURES WITH RATIONALE FROM OWN EXPERIENCES
4. JUSTIFY ANALYSIS TASKS IN TERMS OF TERMINAL BEHAVIOR COMPLEX NEEDS.

THE LEARNER WILL:
1. INTERPRET (TEACHER OR WRITER DEVISED) METHOD ORIENTED CONSTRUCTS NEEDED TO PERFORM SYNTHESIS TASKS
2. IDENTIFY SYNTHESIS TASKS ALREADY MASTERED
3. JUSTIFY SYNTHESIS PROCEDURES WITH RATIONALE FROM OWN EXPERIENCES
4. JUSTIFY SYNTHESIS TASKS IN TERMS OF TERMINAL BEHAVIOR COMPLEX NEEDS.

THE LEARNER WILL:
1. INTERPRET (TEACHER OR WRITER DEVISED) METHOD ORIENTED CONSTRUCTS NEEDED TO PERFORM EVALUATION TASKS
2. IDENTIFY EVALUATION TASKS ALREADY MASTERED
3. JUSTIFY EVALUATION PROCEDURES WITH RATIONALE FROM OWN EXPERIENCES
4. JUSTIFY EVALUATION TASKS IN TERMS OF TERMINAL BEHAVIOR COMPLEX NEEDS.

THE LEARNER WILL:
PERFORM TERMINAL BEHAVIOR COMPLEXES TO SPECIFICATIONS UNDER CONTROLLED CONDITIONS.

RUDIMENTARY TRANSITIONAL OBJECTIVES

	DISCUSSION	CATEGORIES OF TRANSITIONAL OBJECTIVES	SAMPLE TRANSITIONAL OBJECTIVES
RUDIMENTARY TRANSITIONAL OBJECTIVES CONCERNED WITH TERMINAL COMPLEXES	EFFORTS TO KEEP KNOWLEDGE MEANINGFUL, ALIVE, AND AN INTEGRAL PART OF THE DEVELOPING STRUCTURE UNTIL IT SEATS ITSELF IN THE TERMINAL BEHAVIOR COMPLEX INDICATE A TRANSITIONAL CONCERN. THIS MIGHT REQUIRE THE SPECIFICATION OF TRANSITIONAL COMPREHENSION OBJECTIVES FOCUSED ON THESE KNOWLEDGE ELEMENTS.	TERMINAL BEHAVIOR ORIENTED: 1. KNOWLEDGE OF: .1 SPECIFICS .2 WAYS AND MEANS .3 ABSTRACTIONS 2. PSYCHO-MOTOR SKILLS 3. ATTITUDES	1. LEARNER WILL RECALL (AND INTERPRET) THE JUSTIFICATION FOR THE INCLUSION OF SPECIFIC TERMINAL SUB-OBJECTIVES 2. LEARNER WILL PERFORM A MOTOR TASK WHICH RESEMBLES BUT IS NOT IDENTICAL TO THE DESIRED TERMINAL MOTOR BEHAVIOR 3. LEARNER WILL ACTIVELY PARTICIPATE IN ACTIVITIES WHICH HE CAN IDENTIFY AS USEFUL IN HELPING HIM TO REACH THE DESIRED TERMINAL GOALS.
RUDIMENTARY TRANSITIONAL OBJECTIVES CONCERNED WITH OTHER TRANSITIONAL OBJECTIVES	EFFORTS TO STRUCTURE AND JUSTIFY CLASS-ROOM PROCEDURES, REWARD SYSTEMS, LEARNING ACTIVITIES, ETC. REQUIRED KNOWLEDGE AT MANY LEVELS OF THE TAXONOMY. THESE ARE TRANSITIONAL CONCERNS, HOWEVER, IN THAT THEY BECOME NON-FUNCTIONAL WHEN THE TERMINAL BEHAVIORS HAVE BEEN ACHIEVED.	TRANSITIONAL BEHAVIOR ORIENTED: 1. KNOWLEDGE OF: .1 SPECIFICS .2 WAYS AND MEANS .3 ABSTRACTIONS 2. PSYCHO-MOTOR SKILLS 3. ATTITUDES	1. LEARNER WILL RECALL (AND INTERPRET) THE JUSTIFICATION FOR CLASSROOM REGULATIONS REQUIRING A MINIMUM OF UNNECESSARY NOISE AND AIMLESS ACTIVITY IN THE CLASSROOM 2. LEARNER WILL EFFICIENTLY SHARPEN HIS PENCIL (FOLLOW A LINE IN CUTTING WITH SCISSORS, WRITE LEGIBLY, ETC.) AS HE ENGAGES IN ACTIVITIES IN PURSUIT OF THE TERMINAL OBJECTIVES 3. LEARNER WILL REFRAIN FROM DISPLAYS OF ANGER OR OTHER ANTI-SOCIAL EGO-DEFENSIVE ACTIVITIES AS HE ENGAGES IN GROUP ACTIVITIES IN PURSUIT OF TERMINAL OBJECTIVES.

Some Transitional Objectives Typically Associated with the Cells of the Terminally Oriented Design Model *

*See pages 37-38.

The necessity for interruptions in the steady flow of learning may also be greatly reduced by establishing proved methodological procedures that may be reused with only minor variations. Routing procedures may be mapped out and assembled into a manual that might include such topics as group work, library research, laboratory work, writing reports, and similar items. In this way a procedure would need to be programmed only once. After this, a manual reference would be enough. Whether the design and construction of the manual is the responsibility of the designer or the writer of the curriculum materials is dependent upon the number of writers involved in the production of the materials. If several writers were to develop the materials that were based upon the manual, the manual would be the designer's problem. If, however, only a single writer were involved, the manual would be his design.

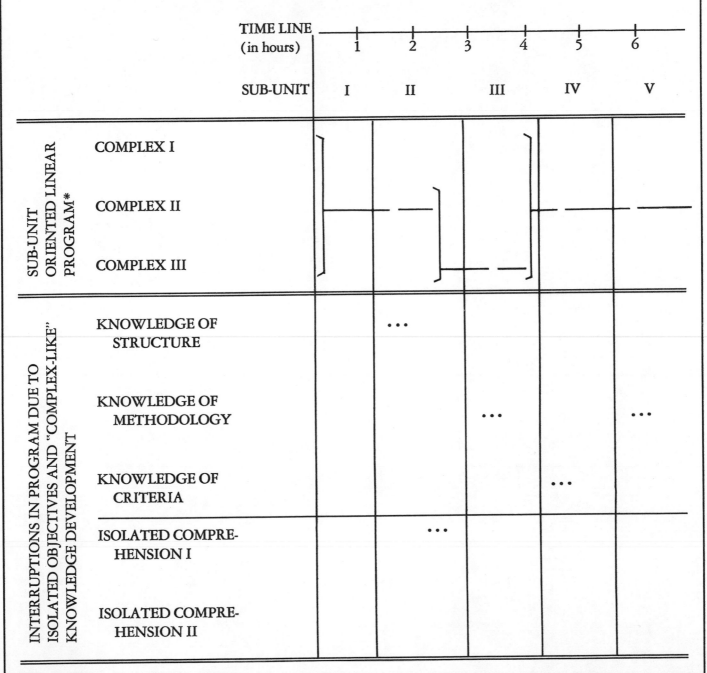

Adapting the Sub-Unit Program of the Terminal Design Model
to Supplementary Curricular Concerns — an Example†

TIME LINE (in hours)		1	2	3	4	5	6
SUB-UNIT		I	II	III		IV	V
SUB-UNIT ORIENTED LINEAR PROGRAM*	COMPLEX I						
	COMPLEX II						
	COMPLEX III						
INTERRUPTIONS IN PROGRAM DUE TO ISOLATED OBJECTIVES AND "COMPLEX-LIKE" KNOWLEDGE DEVELOPMENT	KNOWLEDGE OF STRUCTURE		...				
	KNOWLEDGE OF METHODOLOGY			...			...
	KNOWLEDGE OF CRITERIA					...	
	ISOLATED COMPRE-HENSION I		...				
	ISOLATED COMPRE-HENSION II						

†See page 39.

*The solid line on the chart, paralleling the time line, indicates the "complex" emphasis of the linear program as it develops through the Sub-Units. The breaks in the line indicate that a short program has been inserted (see the dotted line directly below the break).

VI
Using the Model in Curriculum Design

Chapter VI will show how the behavioral-objective focus of Chapter II, the Modified Taxonomy of Chapter III, and the Design Model of Chapter IV can be organized into a procedure of designing curriculum specifications for a set of terminal-behavior objective complexes.

The unit to be developed centers on the following unit terminal behavior complex:

As a result of this unit of instruction the learner will (given the loosely laced shoes on his feet with both strings the same length): Upon request, tie both shoes in twenty seconds with correctly formed bow knots so that the shoes fit snugly.

The procedure outlined defines a routine which can be followed to systematically arrive at a set of specifications. These will enable a writer or a teacher, familiar with the orientation, to write instructional materials or develop an instructional unit which will in turn function as an integral part of a sequence of instruction.

The term "STEP," as used in the following pages, simply indicates a milepost in the procedure rather than a series of discrete routines which must be followed "by the numbers." These step descriptions should be most helpful in pointing out to the designer and writer how the design model should function in a practical situation.

All of the terminal objectives have been classified in terms of their relationship to the unit complex, and as to whether they are "nice to knows" or "needs to knows." These examples should clarify the meaning of the distinctions.

The shoe-tying task is obviously most appropriate for four- or five-year-olds, but this focus has sometimes been ignored in order to produce a well-structured sample objective. The task was selected because every reader has mastered it, because it is a developmental task, because it requires objectives at all levels of the taxonomy, because it can be achieved by most five-year-olds in a one or two week unit of instruction and because it does not require an elaborate development to make the process clear to the reader.

Following are some other simple concerns which might have served almost as well:

sharpening a pencil
making change for a dollar
reading elevations on a contour map
proofreading for correct capitalization
washing a test tube.

More complex groups of behavior complexes to which the procedures can be effectively applied but are too extensive to be used as a clarifying example might focus upon:

predicting the weather from cloud formations
making mathematical estimates using the slide rule
varying sentence patterns in English composition
distinguishing fact from opinion while observing
a political speech.

Steps in Behavior Analysis

Sample Objectives from Shoe-Tying Unit

TAXONOMY LEVEL	NICE TO KNOW (N)	NEEDS TO KNOW (N)	COMPLEX OBJECTIVE (C)	SUB-OBJECTIVE (S)	PREREQUISITE OBJ. (P)	ISOLATED OBJ. (I)
3.0		X	X			
1.11		X		X	X	
1.12	X					X
	X					X
1.21	X					X
1.22	X					X
1.23	X		X			
1.24	X		X			

1. Identify the desired complex of terminal-behavior objectives.

3.0 — As a result of this unit of instruction the child will (given the loosely laced shoes on his feet with both strings the same length):

Upon request, tie both shoes in twenty seconds with correctly formed bow knots so that the shoes fit snugly.

Discussion: In this taxonomy model the application objectives identify the complexes which can then be behaviorally analyzed to provide nearly all the objectives needed to design and construct a curriculum unit and its accompanying materials. Note the importance of the specified "givens." For every new situation described here, the number of sub-objectives which will be derived will be greatly increased. If, for instance, the child were given one long and one short lace, a broken lace, a knotted lace, or an unlaced shoe, the educational problem would be greatly compounded. In this case, the task has been kept simple.

2. Identify the knowledge objectives appropriate to the unit defined by the complex of terminal-behavior objectives (1 above).

As a result of this unit of instruction the child will

1.11 TERMS: recall 85% of the following referents when confronted with the terms (or the terms when presented with the referents):

laces	square knot
eyelets	granny knot
overhand knot	rabbit ears
right hand	snugly
left hand	bow knot

1.12 FACTS: recall the following complete statements of fact when presented with the statement with the italicized portion blank:

a. Untied shoes *cause* many falls.

b. It is more important to specify *the number of eyelets in the shoe than the size of the shoe* when buying shoelaces.

1.21 CONVENTIONS: recall, when asked, that the bow has been one of the major means of fastening shoes for thousands of years.

1.22 TRENDS AND SEQUENCES: recall, when asked, that there is a current trend away from the use of laces, but that it is unlikely that the lace will soon be replaced.

1.23 CLASSIFICATIONS AND CATEGORIES: recall, when asked, that bow knots can be classified as either granny bows or square bows.

1.24 CRITERIA: recall the following criteria when appraising the quality of a "shoe-tie":

a. the shoe should be laced tightly so that no play exists in the lace between the eyelets.

b. the shoes should be secured with a correctly tied bow knot
   1. containing two loops of approximately the same size
   2. tied with a square rather than a granny knot
   3. tied with the ends of the laces at least an inch from the knot
   4. tied so that both loops and ends are well off the floor.

METHODOLOGY: recall, in order, the list of ordered steps and, when given a step, recall the next one on the list:

a. beginning with the eyelet closest to the toe of the shoe, take the slack out of the laces so that the shoe fits snugly

b. put the right lace in the left hand and with the right hand complete an overhand knot and pull it taut

c. make two rabbit ears by doubling the laces so that the ends fall back at least two inches beyond the overhand knot

d. put the left rabbit ear in the right hand and with the left hand complete the overhand knot and pull it tight

e. adjust the loops and ends to correct bow proportions (see criteria).

PRINCIPLES AND GENERALIZATIONS: recall, when asked, that only square bow knots will remain tight.

THEORIES AND STRUCTURES: make the following drawing from memory and recall its key features:

Bow square with foot
All four strings the same length
Off the floor
Laces tight

	N	N	C	S	P	I
1.25	X	X				
1.31					X	
1.32					X	

Discussion: The sophisticated language used in these objectives is geared to the use of the designer and the writer and not the child. These are the knowledge specifications for the curriculum which must be translated by the teachers and writers for children at a specified level of development. Note how the scanning of the categories of the knowledge taxonomy suggests the appropriate specific objectives to one familiar with the complex of terminal-behavior objectives (shoe tying in this case). Note, too, that the objectives classified as "nice to know" cannot be identified by direct inference from the application objectives — they are isolated — but the taxonomy categories actually suggest many of them. It is also likely that the teachers and writers will introduce many other "nice to knows" as they attempt to interest and motivate the learner.

3. Identify the analysis objectives appropriate to the unit defined by the complex of terminal-behavior objectives (1 above).

	N	N	C	S	P	I
4.1		X		X		
		X		X		
		X		X		

As a result of this unit of instruction the child will:

ANALYSIS OF ELEMENTS: Point out, in bow knots in varying stages of completion, the elements to consider in appraising the adequacy of the ties.

ANALYSIS OF RELATIONSHIPS: Point out, in bow knots in varying stages of completion, the possible origins of the knots' shortcomings.

ORGANIZATIONAL PRINCIPLES: Point out, in bow knots of varying stages of completion, the patterns to consider in identifying them as "square" or "granny" bows.

Discussion: Analysis objectives focus on the development of skills in identifying the elements in a problem situation relevant to its solution or elements in a communication relevant to its comprehension or appraisal.

One is concerned with analysis in two phases of shoe-tying. The first deals with a series of appraisals of the situation as the child synthesizes his solution to an actual shoe-tying problem. The second deals with the identification of elements and relationships in the job of evaluating the finished product. The task of identifying the analysis sub-objectives, therefore, requires that one consider both of these concerns as he attends to each of the three analysis categories in the taxonomy. These skills in analysis are tools for performing application, synthesis, and evaluation tasks but serve no ends in themselves. For the most part, the relevant elements being sought in analysis are the "needs to know" knowledge elements.

4. Identify the synthesis objectives appropriate to the unit defined by the complex of terminal-behavior objectives (1 above).

	N	N	C	S	P	I
5.1		X		X		
5.2		X		X		
5.3	X			X		

As a result of this unit of instruction the child will:

PRODUCTION OF A UNIQUE (to him) PERFORMANCE: tie both shoes with correctly formed bow knots so that the shoes fit snugly under unusual conditions (such as when the laces are wet, or short, or especially stiff).

PRODUCTION OF A PLAN OR PROPOSED SET OF OPERATIONS: rephrase and modify the steps in 1.25 to suit his own psycho-motor and cognitive styles. (A transitional objective.)

DERIVE A SET OF ABSTRACT RELATIONS: Discover and formulate the statement that the square knot bow is far superior in holding power to the granny knot bow. (A transitional objective.)

Discussion: Synthesis objectives focus on the task of fabricating a unique performance to meet the demands of a problem or communication situation. In the case of shoe tying, successive refinements in the performance process and minor modifications in the structure of the situation (changing shoes or laces) would tend to make the individual's performance unique to him.

As this unit objective complex defines a routine task to be performed under specified conditions, there are no terminal synthesis objectives clearly in the "needs to know" category. Synthesis objectives would only appear as "nice to know" terminal objectives as in (5.1) or as transitional objectives as in (5.2 and 5.3).

5. Identify the evaluation objectives appropriate to the unit defined by the complex of terminal-behavior objectives (1 above).

As a result of this unit of instruction the child will:

	N	N	C	S	P	I
6.1 JUDGMENTS IN TERMS OF INTERNAL EVIDENCE: none						
6.2 JUDGMENTS IN TERMS OF EXTERNAL EVIDENCE: Appraise the adequacy of a knot-tying performance (providing supporting evidence) at the end of any step defined by the methodology (1.25) in terms of the criteria (1.24).			X	X		

Discussion: Evaluation objectives focus on the task of appraising the adequacy of a performance. In this case the child should be able to make a judgment in appraising the quality of a completed bow knot or a knot at specified stages of development. Internal consistency does not have much meaning here. The external criteria defined in the knowledge objectives (1.24) provide the rationale.

6. Identify the comprehension objectives appropriate to the unit defined by the complex of terminal-behavior objectives (1 above).

As a result of this unit of instruction the child will:

	N	N	C	S	P	I
2.1 TRANSLATION: Give examples of how untied shoes can cause accidents.	X				X	
2.2 INTERPRETATION: Explain why the number of eyelets in a shoe is more important in determining the length of the laces than the size of the shoe.	X				X	
2.3 EXTRAPOLATION: Given the fact that the percentage of laced shoes has steadily decreased over the past forty years, describe the probable future of laced shoes.	X				X	

Discussion: Comprehension objectives focus on the degree of facility one should have in manipulating the knowledge elements. The consideration of these objectives has been put off until step six to let the other objective categories do as much of the job as possible. The reader will note that all of the "needs to know" objectives are integral elements in the complex, and their functions and specifications have been delineated in the Analysis, Synthesis, and Evaluation objectives. This means that the only comprehension objectives which must be specified are in the "nice to know" category where the objective is isolated.

7. Plug all of the above objectives into the cells in the Design Model (or portfolio of objectives).

Discussion: The portfolio format was designed to provide a functional medium for storing, in a readily accessible fashion, all of the terminal objectives appropriate to the construction (or teaching) of a unit of instruction. The major features of the format are:

1. All of the objectives developed in steps 1-6 are included and classified in terms of the taxonomy (but abbreviated so that they can appear on a single chart).

2. The structure has been adapted to complement the Design Model developed in Chapter IV, in that the provision is made for indicating the place in the unit where the objectives will be emphasized.

3. Provision is made for indicating whether the objective is classified as "needs to know" or "nice to know."

4. Provision is made for including and identifying objectives developed in previous units which must be reinforced in the present one.

5. Provision is made for indicating the total number (minimal) of pupil responses to be built into the materials.

6. Provision is made for the writer to tally the responses he has built into the materials (by sub-unit) in an attempt to equal or exceed the specified minimum.

7a. Identify the course or sequence objectives which are directly related to the unit objectives. These can and should be abbreviated.

The child will perform each of the following tasks concerned with personal hygiene and grooming to the degree specified in the objectives of the various units:

1. combing his hair
2. brushing his teeth
3. buttoning his buttons
4. tying his shoes
5. washing his hands
6. caring for his fingernails

Discussion: The presentation of these objectives, in order, gives the writer a perspective as to what has preceded and what will follow the unit. The minimum reinforcement requirements imply that the pupil will perform the task at or near the prescribed proficiency level the specified number of times. The number is arbitrary and might be considered more as a publisher's policy rather than a research-determined absolute. Some standard such as this appears to be necessary and is in conformity with current research in operant conditioning. The number might as a general policy remain constant (say at 10 or 15), or it may be allowed to vary according to the judgment of the designer.

7b. Identify the cognitive-related affective objectives and the cognitive-related motor objectives.

The child will effectively tie both shoes in 20 seconds. (psycho-motor)

The child will, whenever his untied shoe is brought to his attention, tie it. (affective) (This objective is only included as an example and is not a part of this unit.)

Discussion: These categories of objectives have been included because they usually define ingredients essential to the acquisition of a cognitive complex of objectives. Such ingredients are usually far more difficult to establish than the purely cognitive behaviors. The inclusion of 7b, then, forces the writer to provide for a sufficient number of applicable experiences to establish attitudes and motor facility which so often are inadequately considered.

7c. Transfer the objectives developed in steps 1-6 to the portfolio in sufficiently abbreviated forms so that all can be displayed.

See Foldout IV

Discussion: This step is rather a routine one. The knowledge of the facts, classifications of people, dates, etc, have been included because they are common. If "dates" were inappropriate to a unit and colors, exports, or cloth identification were appropriate, they could be substituted. If more room were needed, a page could fold out from the portfolio at right angles to its major axis without hindering its effectiveness. Frequently there will be many blank cells which can be relabeled to extend full cells.

7d. Identify the prerequisite and "needs to know" objectives.

See Foldout IV

7e. Make entry of judgment regarding the minimum number of behavioral responses required for each objective.

See Foldout IV

Discussion: The dimension of this format which is destined to draw the greatest criticism is the designer's judgment of minimum pupil responses to be built into the teaching materials. On the other hand, this is also one of the greatest strengths. The behavioral orientation of this approach insists that an effective performance result from the unit's experiences. This seems more likely to happen if the writer commits himself to the task of providing for the systematic development of the essential knowledge and skills.

As was previously pointed out, this approach to curriculum design and development is geared to a team approach in developing an integrated system of compatible curriculum materials covering broad areas and long-range objectives. Materials can be developed in this way for a conventional self-contained teacher-oriented classroom or for individualized, self-pacing situations. The problem is that the task of developing materials is too great for any single author. When a team approach is used, some of the writer's freedom must be curtailed. The behavioral orientation of this approach tends to greatly restrict the number of "nice to know" objectives, thereby greatly limiting the demands on the writer. The fact that the objectives have already been defined, classified and to some extent sequenced, enables the writer to devote his attention to the learning process rather than subject matter concerns. He can concentrate on motivation, providing for responses and providing for reinforcements.

These portfolio specifications define the structure of the contract entered into by the writer. If the writer feels he has provided adequately for some objectives with fewer than the specified minimum responses in some cases, the burden of proof rests with him.

51

Relevance of the Design Model for Structuring
Systems of Terminal Objectives*

CLASSIFICATION OF ENDS SERVED BY UNIT LEVEL OBJECTIVES	UTILITARIAN ENDS (Includes objectives focused on the acquisition of skills in communicating and problem solving)
EXAMPLES OF DISCIPLINES (that epitomize or could easily be converted to an orientation toward these ends)	Homemaking, auto mechanics, spelling, reading, arithmetic, science
STRENGTHS OF THE "END" ORIENTATION	A practical, beeline approach to the establishing of developmental skills. Appropriate for both individualized or large group instruction.

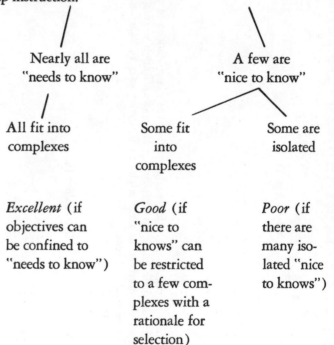

CLASSIFICATION OF ENDS SERVED BY UNIT LEVEL OBJECTIVES	Nearly all are "needs to know"	A few are "nice to know"	
"NICE TO KNOW" VS. "NEEDS TO KNOW" NATURE OF DISCIPLINE'S OBJECTIVES			
DEGREE TO WHICH DISCIPLINES ADAPT THEMSELVES TO BEING ORGANIZED INTO OBJECTIVE COMPLEXES	All fit into complexes	Some fit into complexes	Some are isolated
ADEQUACY OF THE DESIGN MODEL AS A BASIC STRUCTURE FOR CURRICULUM DESIGN	*Excellent* (if objectives can be confined to "needs to know")	*Good* (if "nice to knows" can be restricted to a few complexes with a rationale for selection)	*Poor* (if there are many isolated "nice to knows")

*See pages 56-57.

ACADEMIC ENDS	SELF-ACTUALIZING ENDS
(Include objectives focused on the acquisition of discipline defined skills that are usually, though remotely, related to utilitarian or self-actualizing ends)	(Includes objectives focused on acquisition of soul satisfying skills)

Any discipline from auto mechanics to ancient history, where the mastered behaviors are treated as ends rather than tools	Creative writing, ancient history, chess, religion, piano

A highly abstract approach that is sometimes quite effective with the intelligent and upper socio-economic classes	If the objectives are tailored to the unique personality characteristics of the learner, the pursuit of these ends can be considered quite practical. The approach implies individualized instruction.

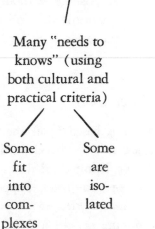

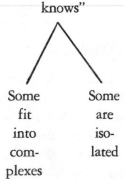

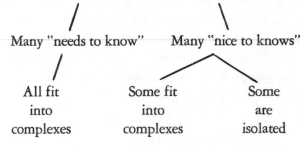

Academic side:

Many "needs to knows" (using both cultural and practical criteria)

- Some fit into complexes
- Some are isolated

Many "nice to knows"

- Some fit into complexes
- Some are isolated

Self-actualizing side:

Many "needs to know"

- All fit into complexes

Many "nice to knows"

- Some fit into complexes
- Some are isolated

Good (if acceptable criteria can be found for the selection of a reasonable number of objective complexes into which the discipline can be divided)	*Poor* (if the discipline's "nice to knows" cannot be integrally organized into a reasonable number of complexes)

Excellent (if objectives can be confined to "needs to knows")	*Good* (if "nice to knows" can be restricted to a few complexes with a rationale for selection)	*Poor* (if there are many isolated "nice to knows")

VII
Specific Guidelines for Using the Design Model

The author has now discussed the need for curriculum design, has presented a model, and has described a general procedure for using it. If the model were to be followed in the development of self-contained, individualized curriculum materials, it would be used by three people, each for a different purpose — the designer, the writer, and the teacher. Here are some guidelines for the three groups.

Use by the Curriculum Designer

Many people, in many education-related roles, are involved in curriculum design. Many have earned their title as public education's curriculum designers by acquiring the needed skills and professional requirements to serve as curriculum coordinators, as members of curriculum committees, or as administrators at local, state, and national levels. Some possess the necessary ability and affect curricula, but lack legitimate authority (such as textbook writers). Some have power to act, but lack "know how." Many are teachers; but all are concerned with the shaping of curricula.

The design model presented in this book will not appeal to all curriculum designers. Its basis is a systematic and scientific orientation and its goal is to enable a designer to "mastermind" the develop-

ment of an extensive curriculum and its supplementary materials to a degree not possible without it. A designer who does not systematically develop specifications will find the model useless. So will a traditionalist.

Dividing a Discipline into Units

Because the unit model is based upon the behavior complex, its usefulness in a field is dependent upon the field's potential for being divided into a reasonable number of behavior complexes. Suppose, for instance, one desires to teach listening skills to fifth graders in two forty-minute periods a week for one year (about 80 sessions, totaling about 55 hours). What would be an ideal number of units (or groups of objective complexes) around which the year's program should be organized? Ideally, a unit should be long enough to tie elementary behaviors into functional units, yet short enough to guarantee that the learner will be able to keep all the learnings in perspective. Again, a unit should be long enough to provide time for the student to identify with objective complexes and participate in the plotting of the course to their mastery. On the other hand, it should be short enough so that the learner does not lose sight of his goals or lose interest.

For a year's work in listening, certainly two units

would be too few (one each semester), and 80 units (one each session) would be too many. One might say that from two to six weeks might be a suitable unit length. This would mean that the year's course of study should contain from six to twelve units. These numbers are arbitrary in that it is the task of the designer to divide the behaviors he is trying to establish into a teachable number of units, each focused on a set of related objective complexes.

To use the model, then, the designer needs a guide for grouping his terminal objectives into an appropriate number of objective complexes. The objective complexes are Application-level objectives and focus on useful application of knowledge and skill components.

Application objectives can be classified under three headings: Problem-Solving, Communicating, and Self-Actualizing. That is to say, cognitive learnings have application in one or more of these areas.

Three questions lead to a reasonable approach to the task of identifying the terminal objective complexes of a discipline:

1. What problem-solving behaviors or skills does the learner need, which are related to the discipline?
2. What communication behaviors or skills does the learner need, which are related to the discipline?
3. What behaviors can the discipline elicit that will help the individual in the process of self-actualization?

The preceding questions serve a real function in the design process because they suggest criteria for both including and excluding objectives. Self-actualization provides a criterion that should be useful in individualizing instruction. One might justify the inclusion of extensive student-initiated historical, philosophical, or religious probes on the grounds that they are essential to the student's development.

Some Disciplines May Require Drastic Restructuring

Traditional mathematics is easily adapted to the model, while traditional history is not. The unanswered question is: could history and some seemingly non-adaptable disciplines be modified to fit the model

without losing their essential characteristics and appeal? Could one use the three criteria to eliminate non-essential historical "nice-to-knows" that contribute nothing to either useful problem-solving behaviors or useful self-actualizing behaviors, and then reorganize the remainder into objective complexes? The author would answer both questions with a qualified "Yes." However, research into this area is needed.

Abandoning Traditional Disciplines

There are some educators who would like to abandon specific traditional disciplines because of their apparent lack of application in the world today. When one considers a discipline by the self-actualizing criterion, one emerges with a new perspective of the meaning of application. Disciplines such as ancient history, Elizabethan drama, and needle point become highly applicable for a few students. An opportunity to develop and apply a skill in one of these areas may be considered a "needs to know" and for some individual may enhance his perception of himself. With this orientation, however, it would seem that many disciplines lend themselves to the cognitive styles of only a few. They have no application for the rest.

A second consideration when weighing the advisability of abandoning a traditional course of study is that it is likely that all the literature pertaining to it is catalogued in the language of the discipline. If it is rejected as a "discipline," a major portion of its language must be retained if its literature or referents are to be used.

The Designer's Specifications to the Writer

The initial and most difficult task of the designer is to identify or devise a series of comprehensive terminal objective complexes that will be the foci for the learning experiences in the unit segments of the course of study. His next major undertaking is task analysis, determining the sub-objectives of the complexes and recording them in the Portfolio of Objectives or a similar structure, based upon the design model.

The designer must then orient his writers to the modified taxonomy and to the design model. This guidebook, together with the exercises in Appendix I, should serve as a useful tool. A personal conference, however, will probably be essential.

The portfolio of objectives, along with the more extensive statements of objectives, constitutes the major portion of the writer's contract. If he fails to meet the specifications, he must rework his material until he does meet them.

If the designer wishes to specify some routine methodological procedures (see Chapter V) to be used by the students throughout a sequence, he should present all the writers with identical specifications.

Use by the Writer

The writer's task is to take the objective specifications prepared by the designer and devise a series of learning experiences that will elicit and reinforce the desired behaviors. As the materials are to be self-pacing and self-directing, the writer must be systematic and thorough. He may develop his own supplementary materials or use those devised by others.

Ideally, the writer should be a systematic, yet creative, teacher with a well-above-average writing ability. One of the strengths of the design model is that the curriculum materials can be produced efficiently by a team of educators who are capable, but not necessarily uniquely qualified in their field. The paramount criterion is that the writer be a methodical and creative teacher. If his writing is high average, it can be edited.

The writer's first task is to master the modified taxonomy, the design model, and the portfolio,[9] to the extent that he could, given a simple terminal objective complex — say, brushing the teeth — accomplish the following:

1. Correctly identify a related objective in each of the six major categories of the taxonomy and explain the relationship between the objectives in terms of the modified taxonomy.
2. Correctly place the objectives he has identified into the portfolio and then into the de-

[9]These skills are developed in Chapters II-V and the accompanying exercises in Appendix I. A publisher might route all prospective writers through the readings and exercises.

sign model (see Appendix II, Foldouts III and IV).
3. Convert his two-dimensional model to a linear program (see chart on page 43).

Armed with the skills defined above, the writer must then familiarize himself with the objectives specified by the designer in the portfolio to the extent that he can:

1. Identify and justify the relationships between the sub-objectives and the objective complexes.
2. Explain, in terms of the objectives, the educational problems to be overcome in each of the sub-units (see sub-model, page 40).

His next task is to determine the teaching strategy he will use to overcome the two problems stated above. Some of these may well have been delineated by the designer, such as group discussion techniques or laboratory techniques. For the most part, however, the selection is up to him. His basic problem is to isolate and program the mainstream of experiences that will lead the learner to achieving the terminal objective complexes. With this orientation, he is left to his own resources.

Use by the Teacher

For the teacher who desires to play the role of a designer or writer, guidelines appeared earlier in the chapter. This section is a guide for teachers using self-pacing materials based upon the design model in individualized or small group instruction. Just as it is possible to drive an automobile without knowledge of the structure of the vehicle, so it is possible to use well developed, self-pacing materials without knowledge of them. The professional driver and the diagnosticians, however, need more knowledge. When the vehicle ceases to function efficiently, the riders, whether they be drivers or students, need help. If the diagnostician knows the vehicle, the treatment will be appropriate and efficiently managed. If he does not, he will administer treatment in a trial and error fashion, which is both time-consuming and frustrating to all.

The author feels that whenever students are using these self-pacing materials, the teacher should have the portfolios of relevant objectives at his fingertips. He should also have become familiar enough with the portfolio and its structure so that he can quickly perceive the relationships between the various sub-objectives and the objective complexes of a unit.

Chapters II-V, and the exercises in Appendix I that accompany them, should serve to orient the teacher to the structure of the materials. With this as a background, one can quickly survey and appraise a portfolio geared to a specific unit.

Individualized instruction usually requires periodic individual conferences with the learner. The portfolio structures the conference. With the portfolio before him, the teacher can pinpoint the learner's present position and the degree of proficiency he should possess for each of the terminal objectives. With a few well directed, objective-oriented questions, the teacher can diagnose the student's strengths and weaknesses and institute remedial procedures.

Without the statement of objectives, these materials would probably be indistinguishable from other good self-pacing materials. Their strength lies in the fact that their structure can be easily communicated, and in the fact that the teacher is assured that the objectives are comprehensive and systematically reinforced. These strengths, moreover, enable the teacher to feel that he is capable of communicating with the learner at any time and that every learner is involved in meaningful, quickly identifiable activities that are objective centered.

The Relevance of the Design Model for Schools Today

The general theme of this book is that the modified taxonomy can provide a structure for making comprehensive specifications of end objectives for the use of writers of curriculum materials and for teachers. These objectives can then be inserted into the design model to provide for the general sequencing of objectives for treatment during instruction to insure that they will all receive sufficient emphasis.

The application of the modified taxonomy and the design model are dependent upon two important factors: First, the discipline must lend itself to a division into behavior complexes; secondly, the user must be willing to accept the idea that the "needs to know" objectives derived from the objective complexes provide an adequate orientation to the discipline.

Looking at the chart directly ahead of this chapter, note that three orientations to stating objectives for an instructional unit are delineated. The first, labeled "Utilitarian," centers on the two Application objective foci used throughout the book—problem-solving and communicating. If one could accept the position that all the cognitive aims of the school could be classified under these headings, one's concerns would be "utilitarian." This orientation is probably most suited to an educator with strong science leanings.

The second orientation, "Academic," relates to a more traditional position, a discipline that has been shaped over a long period of time. The elements of the discipline may, or may not, have originally focused on practical concerns. Currently, however, they are thought of as integral parts of the body of knowledge. It is usually assumed that, when the discipline has been mastered by an individual, he will then be able to perform countless practical tasks. This assumption, however, is seldom examined. Some educators within the academic orientation use a scientific approach to the *transfer* of training and get quite satisfactory results. But if their evaluation procedures focus on the discipline rather than the application, one can, without reservations, call them Academic.

The third orientation, "Self-Actualizing," includes those objectives geared to the development of a dynamic, integrated self — the major elements of which are at least partially under the cognitive control of the individual. Courses such as mental health, modern dance, music appreciation, or creative writing could clearly have a Self-Actualizing focus. This orientation is very similar to Utilitarian in that it deals with behaviors directly related to the individual and his adjustment to his environment. It has been kept separate, however, because an educator need not accept both as legitimate ends of education. Note, too, that the Utilitarian and Self-Actualizing orientations, when considered together, account for most of the emphasis of the academic position — from the clearly practical to the "knowing for the sake of knowing."

From these three approaches — Utilitarian, Academic, and Self-Actualizing — most educators should be able to select a position with which they identify.

The chart then separates the "needs to knows" from the "nice to knows" for each of the approaches. The Utilitarian and Self-Actualizing approaches are almost identical in their development and consist essentially of "needs to knows." If the learner can master the "needs to know" complexes, he has mastered the essentials of the discipline. If a "nice to know" complex is inserted occasionally, with a rationale to justify it, it can be processed in a manner similar to the other complexes. Because both approaches are oriented toward practical applications, these applications *are* the complexes and there is little else in the form of isolated objectives needed by the frugal educator. If, however, the educator claiming this position clings to the traditional niceties of the discipline, the design model will be of little use to him.

Each column is then summarized with evaluative statements, indicating the applicability of the design model to the orientation. Such evaluations depend upon the characteristics of the discipline and the biases of the educator.

The Self-Actualizing approach seems to have a limited application in public schools because of the extensive need for individualized materials and guidance. If suitable materials were developed, they would probably be well received.

Considering the Academic approach, one can see that the "needs to know" complexes are unlikely to include most objectives of a discipline. In addition, most traditional disciplines contain many "needs to know" isolated objectives. As none of the isolated objectives are attached to complexes, no provision is made for their systematic treatment. With many disciplines, therefore, the model would only complicate matters.

Some academic disciplines, however, lend themselves to the design model orientation — as arithmetic or handwriting. Hence, the "good" appraisal criterion is given at the bottom of the academic column on the chart. If most of the objectives of the discipline can be incorporated into a reasonable number of objective complexes, the design model is applicable.

The chart should be useful as a guide in appraising the degree to which a discipline would yield to the design model. The initial task would be to classify the discipline into one of the three approach categories. If it were classified as Utilitarian or Self-Actualizing and its essential objectives could be grouped into a reasonable number of complexes, the model would be applicable. If this proves to be impossible, then the model will not apply.

If the discipline were classified as Academic, one might first appraise the feasibility of reorganizing it into one of the other approaches (or, possibly, by using a combination of the two approaches). If this could not be done, then the question would be, "Can the objectives of the discipline be grouped into objective complexes with very few isolated objectives remaining?" If the answer be, "Yes," then the design model would be applicable to such a discipline. If "No," the model would not apply.

Glossary

Affective domain.   A classification of educational objectives characterized by their focus on the development of attitudes, beliefs, and values. *See* Domain.*

Analysis (objectives).   Modified taxonomy category (4.0). Concerned with objectives which focus on the development of skills identifying the elements in a problem situation relevant to its solution, or elements in a communication relevant to its comprehension or appraisal.

Analysis of Elements.   Modified taxonomy sub-category (4.1). Concerned with objectives related to the identification of relevant elements in an Application (3.0) task situation which are needed for the performance of the task.

Analysis of Organizational Principles.   Modified taxonomy sub-category (4.3). Concerned with objectives related to the identification of relevant organizational principles in an Application task situation which are needed for the performance of the task.

Analysis of Relationships.   Modified taxonomy sub-category (4.2). Concerned with objectives related to the identification of relevant relationships which are needed for the performance of an Application (3.0) task.

*Capitalized terms appearing in the definitions have been defined in the glossary.

Application (objectives).   Modified taxonomy category (3.0). Concerned with objectives which focus on the use of abstractions in particular and concrete situations. (These can focus on Problem-solving, Communicating, or Self-actualization).

Behavior analysis.   The process by which a complex behavior is broken down into teachable components.

Behavioral objective.   An objective conforming to a format for stating an educational goal in terms of the behavior to be elicited.

Bloom Taxonomy.   *See* Taxonomy.

Cognitive domain.   A classification of educational objectives characterized by their dependence upon the manipulation of language symbols (thinking).

Communication.   The cognitive process by which language symbols are manipulated to transmit ideas between people and groups. Learning tasks focused on the mastery of the language and techniques of communicating provide the focus for many objective complexes at the unit, course and sequence levels.

Comprehension (objectives).   Modified taxonomy category (2.0). Concerned with objectives which define the degree of facility one should have in translating, interpreting, and extrapolating recallable knowledge.

Curriculum. Those sequenced experiences that the school consciously and purposefully provides for the learner, directed toward the achievement of terminal objectives.

Derivation of a Set of Abstract Relations. Modified taxonomy sub-category (5.3). Concerned with Synthesis objectives which require the combining of elements into a new product.

Design model. The Drumheller model for designing curricula from objectives based on the Modified taxonomy. The model serves as the focus for the book and appears in Foldout III, Appendix II.

Discipline. The integral collection of related behavior complexes of a field of specialization. (For example: dishwashing and mathematics are disciplines).

Domain. A sphere of activity. According to Bloom, all educational objectives can be classified into one of three spheres: the cognitive domain, the affective domain, and the psycho-motor domain.

End objective. *Same as* Terminal objective.

Evaluation (objectives). Modified taxonomy category (6.0). Concerned with objectives which focus on the task of appraising the adequacy of a performance.

Extrapolation. Modified taxonomy sub-category (2.3). Concerned with Comprehension objectives related to the extension of given data to determine implications, consequences, corollaries of facts, etc.

Hierarchical. A characteristic of the structure of the Bloom taxonomy based on evidence showing that the learner tends to master the lower level objectives before he masters the higher level objectives.

Interpretation. Modified taxonomy sub-category (2.2). Concerned with Comprehension objectives related to the summarization of a simple communication or problem situation by reordering or rearranging the original.

Isolated objective. An objective which is not an integral part of an objective complex.

Judgments in terms of External Criteria. Modified taxonomy sub-category (6.2). Concerned with Evaluation objectives related to the appraisal of a product with reference to selected or remembered criteria.

Judgments in terms of Internal Evidence. Modified taxonomy sub-category (6.1). Concerned with Evaluation objectives related to the appraisal of a product from such evidence as logical accuracy, consistency, and other internal criteria.

Knowledge of Classifications and Categories. Modified taxonomy sub-category (1.23). Concerned with objectives related to the recall of knowledge of the classes, sets, divisions, and arrangements which are basic for a given subject field.

Knowledge of Conventions. Modified taxonomy sub-category (1.21). Concerned with objectives related to the recall of knowledge of usages, styles, practices, and forms which are agreed upon within a field.

Knowledge of Criteria. Modified taxonomy sub-category (1.24). Concerned with objectives related to the recall of knowledge of the rule or test by which facts, principles, opinions, and conduct are tested or judged.

Knowledge of Methodology. Modified taxonomy sub-category (1.25). Concerned with objectives related to the recall of knowledge of the method of inquiry, technique, and procedures employed in a particular field as well as those employed in investigating particular problems and phenomena.

Knowledge (objective). Modified taxonomy category (1.0). Concerned with objectives related to the recall of specifics, universals, methods, and processes or of a pattern, structure or setting. The psychological processes of remembering.

Knowledge of Principles and Generalizations. Modified taxonomy sub-category (1.31). Concerned with objectives related to the recall of knowledge of particular abstractions which summarize observations of phenomena.

Knowledge of Specifics. Modified taxonomy classification (1.1). A sub-grouping of knowledge objectives concerned with the recall of specific isolated bits of information.

Knowledge of Specific Facts. Modified taxonomy sub-category (1.12). Concerned with objectives related to the recall of knowledge of dates, events, persons, places, etc.

Knowledge of Terminology. Modified taxonomy sub-category (1.11). Concerned with objectives related to the recall of knowledge of the referents for specific symbols or the recall of symbols for specific referents.

Knowledge of Theories and Structures. Modified taxonomy sub-category (1.32). Concerned with objectives related to the recall of knowledge of the body of principles and generalizations which are interrelated to form a theory or structure.

Knowledge of Trends and Sequences. Modified taxonomy sub-category (1.22). Concerned with objectives related to the recall of knowledge of processes, directions, and movements of phenomena with respect to time.

Knowledge of the Universals and Abstractions in a Field. Modified taxonomy classification (1.3). A grouping of knowledge objectives concerned with the major schemes and patterns by which phenomena and ideas are organized.

Knowledge of Ways and Means of Dealing with Specifics. Modified taxonomy classification (1.2). A sub-grouping of knowledge objectives concerned with ways of organizing, studying, judging, criticizing, and inquiring.

Learning. A change in behavior resulting from experience.

Means objective. *Same as* Transitional objective.

Modified taxonomy. *See* Taxonomy.

Module. A standardized unit segment of instruction. In the Design model orientation a "Unit" module is used. Equivalent unit modules can be adapted to different cognitive styles.

"Needs to know." An objective which stems from a developmental task and is necessary for adequate development of the individual — (socially, vocationally, economically, etc.).

"Nice to know." An objective which is considered either by the educator or society as desirable, but cannot be justified in terms of a developmental task.

Objective. *Same as* Behavioral objective.

Portfolio (of objectives). A foldout chart following a prescribed format which enables the viewer to see all of the terminal objectives of a unit at a glance. The format also provides for showing the relationship between the objectives and their position of emphasis in the programmed instruction.

Prerequisite objective. A behavior which should have been achieved prior to the undertaking of a particular objective complex.

Problem-solving. The cognitive process involving the symbolic manipulation of elements in a blocked task to overcome the blocking. This is the major focus of most objective complexes at the unit, course, or sequence level.

Production of a Plan or Proposed Set of Operations. Modified taxonomy sub-category (5.2). Concerned with Synthesis objectives related to the development of a plan or proposal.

Production of a Unique Communication. Modified taxonomy sub-category (5.1). Concerned with Synthesis objectives related to the development of a communication in which the writer or speaker attempts to convey ideas or feelings to others.

Psycho-motor domain. The classification of educational objectives characterized by their focus on the development of motor behaviors. *See* Domain.

Rudimentary level objective. The Knowledge, Affective and Psycho-motor Sub-objectives of an Objective complex.

Rudimentary objectives. The Knowledge, Psycho-motor and Affective components of Objective complexes. For the most part, these objectives can be considered as conditioned responses.

Self-actualizing. The quality in an experience through which one realizes his potentialities. A characteristic of an Objective complex which can qualify it as a terminal unit, course or sequence objective. It refers to Kurt Goldstein's notion that the normal individual constantly behaves in a manner which tends to enhance his image of himself. An Objective complex focused on the cognitive task of nurturing the student's ability to modify or control his image of himself is said to have a "self-actualizing" focus.

Sub-objective. An objective derived through the process of behavior analysis from an Objective complex.

Sub-unit. A strategic, learning-oriented segment of a unit of instruction. In the "Design model" five sub-units are specified. *See* Sub-unit level objective.

Sub-unit level objective. A sub-objective of a unit's terminal objective complex classified according to the Modified taxonomy at either the Analysis, Synthesis or Evaluation levels. The curriculum writer or teacher might, at times, also consider the unit-objective complexes as sub-unit level objectives.

Synthesis (objectives). Modified taxonomy category (5.0). Concerned with objectives which focus on the task of fabricating a unique performance to meet the demands of a problem or communication situation.

Taxonomy. A classification system whose structure defines the relationships between the categories. Bloom taxonomy: The taxonomy defined in *Taxonomy of Educational Objectives: Handbook I, Cognitive Domain.*
Modified taxonomy: Drumheller's revision of the

Bloom taxonomy.

Terminal objectives. A behavioral goal which is considered to be an "end" objective of a unit, course, or sequence.

Transitional objective. A behavioral objective which plays a supporting role in the reaching of a terminal objective. It describes a behavior which is a "means" to an "end." When the terminal objective is reached, the transitional behavior is no longer necessary.

Translation. Modified taxonomy sub-category (2.1).

Concerned with Comprehension objectives related to the part-for-part paraphrasing of a communication or restating of a problem.

Unit. A segment of instruction which focuses on the attainment of one or more related terminal-objective complexes.

Unit level objective. The terminal objective complexes upon which the sub-objectives of the unit are based. In units containing isolated comprehension terminal objectives, these might also be considered in this category.

References

Ayers, J. Douglas. "Justification of Bloom's taxonomy by factor analysis." Paper read at the Annual American Educational Research Association Convention, Chicago, Illinois, February, 1966.

Ayers, Leonard P. *Ayers' Measuring Scale for Handwriting.* (Gettysburg Edition). New York: Russell Sage Foundation.

Bloom, Benjamin S. (ed.) *Taxonomy of Educational Objectives: Handbook I, Cognitive Domain.* New York: David McKay, 1956.

Cox, Richard C. "The first decade." Paper read at the Annual American Educational Research Association, Chicago, Illinois, February, 1966.

Cox, Richard C. and Gordon, John M. "Validation and uses of the *Taxonomy of Educational Objectives: Cognitive Domain."* A mimeographed select and annotated bibliography. University of Pittsburgh, 1966.

Gagne, Robert M. Paper presented at the National Symposium on Research in Programmed Instruction. Washington, D.C., 1963.

Goldstein, Kurt. "Organismic approach to the problem of motivation." *Trans. New York Academy of Sciences, 9,* 1947, 218-30.

Havighurst, Robert J. *Human Development and Education.* New York: Longmans and Green, 1953.

Hill, Wilhelmina. *Unit Planning and Teaching in Elementary Social Studies.* Washington, D.C.: U.S. Dept. of Health, Education, and Welfare, Dept. of Education, 1963, 1-3.

Kinney, Lucien B. "Operational plan in the classroom." *School and Society, 68,* September 4, 1948, 145-148.

Kapfer, Miriam B. *Behavioral Objectives in Curriculum Development — Selected Readings and Bibliography.* Englewood Cliffs, New Jersey: Educational Technology Publications, 1971.

Krathwohl, David R. "Stating objectives appropriately for program, for curriculum and for instructional materials development." *Journal of Teacher Education,* 1965, (1), 83-92.

Krathwohl, David R., Bloom, Benjamin, and Masia, Bertram. *Taxonomy of Educational Objectives, Handbook II: Affective Domain.* New York: David McKay, 1964.

Lawrence, Gordon D. "Analysis of teacher-made tests in social studies according to the *Taxonomy of Educational Objectives."* (Clarmontiana Collection) Claremont College, Claremont, California. Unpublished Masters Thesis.

Lessinger, Leon M. "Test building and test banks through the use of the *Taxonomy of Educational Objectives." California Journal of Educational Research.* 1963, 14 (5), 195-201.

Maslow, A. *Motivation and Personality.* New York: Harper, 1954.

McGuire, Christine. "Research in the process approach to the construction and to analysis of medical examinations." *National Council on Measurement in Education Yearbook.* 1963, 20, 7-16.

Milholland, John E. "An empirical examination of the categories of the *Taxonomy of Educational Objectives: Cognitive Domain.*" Paper read at the Annual American Educational Research Association Convention, Chicago, Illinois, February, 1966.

Sanders, Norris. "A taxonomy-based rationale for the improvement of the quality and variety of classroom questions, assignments, and examinations." Paper read at the Annual American Educational Research Association Convention, Chicago, Illinois, February, 1966.

Scannell, Dale P., and Stellwagen, Walter R. "Teaching and testing for degrees of understanding." *California Journal of Instructional Improvement,* 1960, *3* (1), 8-14.

Stanley, Julian C., and Bolton, Dale. See book review section of *Educational and Psychological Measurement,* 1957, *17,* 631-634.

Stevens, Godfrey D. "Taxonomy in special education for children with body disorders." Department of Special Education and Rehabilitation, University of Pittsburgh, 1965.

Stoker, Howard W. "An emerging trend in achievement testing." Paper read at the Annual meeting of the Florida Educational Research Association, 1964.

Stoker, Howard W. and Kropp, R. P. "Measurement of cognitive processes." *Journal of Educational Measurement,* 1964, *1* (1), 39-42.

Svitavsky, Leo E. "Avowed and Operative Objectives of College Courses in Music as General Education in 10 Colleges of the State University of New York." Ed. D. Thesis. Columbia U., 1966.

Travers, Robert M. W. *How to Make Achievement Tests.* New York: Odyssey Press, 1950.

Tyler, Louise L. *"The Taxonomy of Educational Objectives: Cognitive Domain* — its use in evaluating programmed instruction." *California Journal of Educational Research,* 1966, *17* (1), 26-32.

Tyler, Louise L. and Okumu, Laura J. "A beginning step: a system for analyzing courses in teacher education." *Journal of Teacher Education,* 1965, *16* (4), 438-444.

Wood, Jean Marie. "A survey of objectives for teacher education." Prepared for the Commission on Teacher Education Association for Supervision and Curriculum Development. San Bernardino City School System, San Bernardino, California, 1960.

Zinn, Karl L. "The use of the taxonomy and computer assistance in assembling sets of objectives, test items, and diagnostic test sequences." Paper read at the Annual American Educational Research Association Convention, Chicago, Illinois, February, 1966.

Appendix I
Learner Interaction Exercises

The following exercises are designed for the reader who would like to develop a proficiency in the behaviors discussed in chapters II through IV.* The format for each chapter is:

    1. A brief exercise, considering a programmed discussion question, involves the reader in a survey of the chapter.

    2. The reader evaluates his work by using model responses and scoring keys that appear frequently.

*Some suggestions for adapting these exercises for use in workshops are given on page 103 of Appendix I.

    3. A summary describes the essential skills needed for the performance of the terminal complexes.

    4. The remaining exercises establish the behaviors of the sub-objectives.

Since the exercises are programmed to include the essential concepts and skills, the learner should perform the tasks in their sequential order for best results.

Chapter II
Exercise I

1. In behavioral terms, write what you think is the key *terminal objective complex* of this chapter by completing the statement below. (If necessary, refer to pages 10-13).

As a result of the experiences encountered in Chapter II, the learner will:

2. List points that prove that your statement is an *objective complex*. (Pages 11-12).

3. Quote words from your objective that indicate it meets each of the following criteria for an adequate behavioral objective:

a. Statement describes what learner will do. (Pages 13-14)

a. _____

_____

b. Essential characteristics of desired behaviors are explicitly stated. (Pages 13-14)

b. _____

_____

_____

c. Conditions under which behavior is expected are specified. (Pages 13-14)

c. _____

_____

4. Briefly list points that prove that your objective measures up to each of the following criteria for an adequately stated objective:

a. Expected behavior is within the ability   a. _____
level of the learner. (Pages 13-14)

                                        _____

b. Expected behaviors can be observed.   b. _____
(Pages 13-14)

                                        _____

c. Expected behaviors can be evaluated.   c. _____
(Pages 13-14)

                                        _____

5. If you are not now satisfied with your objective statement, revise it below.

Self-Evaluation Suggestions:

The author's version of the objective complexes of the chapter are stated below. The learner (or in-service teacher) will:

1. Appraise statements of objectives in his field of specialization, written either by himself or others, in terms of the six criteria (listed below).

2. Write statements of objectives in his field of specialization consistent with the six criteria (listed below).

3. Classify a list of objectives in terms of the functional categories of behavioral objectives (listed below).

Two frames of reference provide the rationales for the performance of the preceding tasks:

1. Regarding Objective Complexes 1 and 2:

Criteria for Appraising the Adequacy of Statements of Behavioral Objectives

A. Statement describes what learner will do. (Page 14)

B. Essential characteristics of desired behaviors are explicitly stated. (Page 14)

C. Conditions under which behavior is expected are specified. (Page 14)

D. Expected behavior is within the ability level of the learner. (Page 14)

E. Expected behavior can be observed. (Page 14)

F. Expected behavior can be evaluated. (Page 14)

2. Regarding Objective 3:

Functional Classifications of Behavioral Objectives (Pages 11-13)

A. End Objectives (Terminal)

   1. Prerequisite Objectives

   2. Objective Complexes

   3. Sub-Objectives

   4. Isolated Objectives

B. Means Objectives (Transitional)

   1. Prerequisite Objectives

   2. Objective Complexes

   3. Sub-Objectives

   4. Isolated Objectives

Chapter II
Exercise II

Appraise each of the following statements of objectives in terms of the criteria given previously.

Directions:

1. Place a + in the space provided if the objective meets the criterion or a — if it is inadequate.

2. After five statements have been appraised, turn the page and check responses.

3. Repeat the procedure and check responses after statement 10.

4. Repeat procedure and check responses after statement 15.

	Identifies desired behavior.	Explicitly describes what learner will do.	Describes conditions under which performance will occur.	Expected behavior can be observed.	Expected behavior can be evaluated.
The learner will:					
1. Write his name.					
2. Understand world interdependence.					
3. Count accurately when playing classroom number games.					
4. Identify and classify the propaganda devices used in syndicated columns on the editorial page of the local paper (based on structure developed in class).					
5. Sing the correct words when the national anthem is played in school assemblies.					
6. Know his full name and address when asked by teacher.					
7. As a player, be honest in calling tennis shots falling near line.					
8. Name the planets of the solar system in order — from the sun — when asked by the teacher.					
9. Identify relevant element in mathematic word problems when extraneous data are included.					
10. Have a better understanding of the federal system of checks and balances.					
11. Name six carnivorous animals.					
12. Swim the length of the school pool in less than one minute, without artificial support, starting from an immersed position at the deep end of the pool.					
13. Think clearly when called upon in class to think on his feet.					
14. Respond orally and accurately to multiplication flash cards from 1 x 1 = ..., through 12 x 12 = ..., when cards are presented to him in class.					
15. Cover his mouth every time he sneezes.					

Chapter II
Exercise III

Place an (X) to the left of the objective complex below with which you are most familiar. This complex will serve as a focus of the remaining exercises. If none of these appeals to you, write an appropriate one in the space provided at number 5.

(   ) 1. Mathematics (sixth grade): The student will, when asked by the teacher, divide a decimal (up to four decimal places) by a decimal (up to four decimal places) without error, using paper and pencil.

(   ) 2. Science (eighth grade): The student will propose a written plan consistent with the soil conservation criteria developed in the (eighth grade) text for the rehabilitation of an eroded abandoned farm in the vicinity of the school.

(   ) 3. Language Arts (ninth grade): The student will identify the biases betrayed by selected "letters to the editor" focused upon a single referent and explain how the biases prevent communication and agreement on the part of the writers.

(   ) 4. Social Studies (fifth, eighth, or eleventh grade): The student will identify the major political, economic and social causes of the American Civil War and explain why a peaceful settlement was impossible.

(   ) 5.

Directions:

1. Spaces are provided below for the development of objectives relevant to the selected objective complex above. It is expected that your responses will meet the six criteria for an adequate behavioral objective. (The back of the preceding page may be used as a worksheet.)

2. The learner is expected to appraise his finished product with the appropriate word (good, fair, poor).

1	+ — — + —
2	— — — — —
3	+ + + + +
4	+ + + + +
5	+ + + + +
6	— — + — —
7	— — + — —
8	+ + + + +
9	+ + + + +
10	— — — — —
11	+ + — + +
12	+ + — + +
13	— — + — —
14	+ + + + +
15	+ + + + +

(See page 73.)

Directions:

Appraise the adequacy of each statement (good, fair, poor) on the grid at the right below.

1. In the space below, write a terminal sub-objective that may be included in a unit focused upon the terminal objective complex you selected.

2. In the space below, write a transitional objective complex that may be included in a unit focused upon your terminal objective complex.

3. In the space below, write a terminal isolated objective that may be included in a unit focused upon your terminal objective complex.

4. In the space below, write a transitional sub-objective that may be included in a unit focused upon your terminal objective complex.

5. In the space below, write a terminal prerequisite objective that may be included in a unit focused upon your terminal objective complex.

Tells what learner will do.	Explicitly describes what learner will do.	Describes conditions under which performance will occur.	Expected behavior within ability level of learner.	Expected behavior can be observed.	Expected behavior can be evaluated.	Does it belong in the category requested?

Chapter III
Exercise I (Overview)
The Modified Taxonomy

This is an exercise to orient the reader to the general structure of the modified taxonomy. Your task is to take the terminal objective complex selected in Exercise III (Chapter II) and write an objective appropriate to each of the six major taxonomy categories. Your objectives should be derived through an analysis of the selected complex.

Suggestions: Before beginning the exercise, scan the following references and use them when necessary:
1. Bloom Foldout I
2. Modified Taxonomy Foldout II
3. Chapter II (pages 10 to 15)
4. Chapter III (pages 17 to 29)

Note that the exercise sheet follows the format of the modified taxonomy foldout. Remember, only one objective in each category is called for. Objectives should conform to behavioral criteria.

1. *Knowledge Objective*

----

2. *Comprehension Objective*

Classify this objective:

Nice to Know ( )

Needs to Know ( )

Is it duplicated in 4-6?

Yes ( ), No ( )

Terminal Objective Complex.
(Copy your complex in the space below. If you wish, you can restrict the scope of the given complex, but this is not necessary.)

----

3. *Application Objective*

----

4. *Analysis Objective*

----

5. *Synthesis Objective*

----

6. *Evaluation Objective*

----

1. Do your objective statements meet the six criteria for acceptable objectives (page 14)?

2. Except for "comprehension," are all the listed objectives essential to the mastery of the terminal complex?

3. Does your classification of these objectives conform to the criteria found on pages 17-21 of Chapter III?

The following flow chart summarizes the procedures followed in Exercise I and points the way to the more refined procedures required in Exercise II:

BEHAVIOR ANALYSIS PROCEDURE BASED ON THE MODIFIED TAXONOMY OF OBJECTIVES

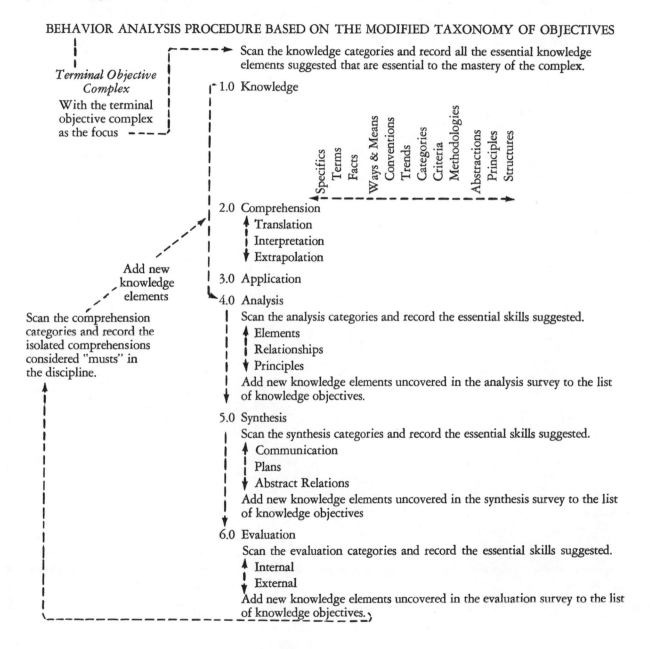

Chapter III
Exercise II

The learner will identify an objective for each of the 21 cells of the taxonomy relevant to his selected objective complex. The flow chart on the preceding page should serve to orient him to the task. Pages 23-25 of Chapter III illustrate the procedure with examples.

Step I. Classify the objectives you developed in Exercise I that met the evaluation criteria by re-writing them in the appropriate cells below. (Modify them if necessary.)

Step II. Follow the prescribed routine to fill the remainder of the 21 cells with *A SAMPLE* objective.

Note: It probably will be necessary to include other than "needs to know" objectives to fill all 21 cells. As this is an exercise in classifying, analyzing, and writing objectives using the whole taxonomy, try to fill all the cells. A place has been provided where you can label your response as either "needs to know" or "nice to know." Use the "nice to know" only when the "needs to know" cannot be identified.

	Needs to Know	Nice to Know

1.0 *KNOWLEDGE OBJECTIVES*

KNOWLEDGE OF SPECIFICS:
1.11 *KNOWLEDGE OF TERMS:* The student will:

1.12 *KNOWLEDGE OF FACTS:* The student will:

KNOWLEDGE OF WAYS AND MEANS OF DEALING WITH SPECIFICS:
1.21 *KNOWLEDGE OF CONVENTIONS:* The student will:

1.22 *KNOWLEDGE OF TRENDS AND SEQUENCES:* The student will:

1.23 *KNOWLEDGE OF CLASSIFICATIONS AND CATEGORIES:* The student will:

1.24 *KNOWLEDGE OF CRITERIA:* The student will:

1.25 *KNOWLEDGE OF METHODOLOGY:* The student will:

KNOWLEDGE OF ABSTRACTIONS:
1.31 *KNOWLEDGE OF PRINCIPLES AND GENERALIZATIONS:*
The student will:

1.32 KNOWLEDGE OF THEORIES AND STRUCTURES:
The student will:

2.0 *COMPREHENSION OBJECTIVES*

2.1 *TRANSLATION:* The student will:

2.2 *INTERPRETATION:* The student will:

2.3 *EXTRAPOLATION:* The student will:

3.0 *APPLICATION:* The student will:

4.0 *ANALYSIS OBJECTIVES*

4.1 *ELEMENTS:* The student will:

4.2 *RELATIONSHIPS:* The student will:

4.3 *ORGANIZATIONAL PRINCIPLES:* The student will:

5.0 *SYNTHESIS OBJECTIVES*

5.1 *PRODUCTION OF A UNIQUE COMMUNICATION:*
The student will:

5.2 *PRODUCTION OF A PLAN OR PROPOSED SET OF
OPERATIONS:* The student will:

5.3 *DERIVATION OF A SET OF ABSTRACT RELATIONS:*
The student will:

Needs to Know	Nice to Know

6.0 *EVALUATION OBJECTIVES*

6.1 *JUDGMENTS IN TERMS OF INTERNAL EVIDENCE:*
The student will:

6.2 JUDGMENTS IN TERMS OF EXTERNAL EVIDENCE:
The student will:

Suggestions for Evaluating Objectives in Exercise II:

Compare each objective with the category definition, pages 17-21 of Chapter III, and with the example objective presented in Foldout II.

Remember that the six criteria for adequately formulated objectives still apply.

Because it is so easy to deceive one's self, try to exchange responses to Exercise II with another learner. Follow the same procedure.

Needs to Know	Nice to Know

Chapter IV
Exercise I
The Drumheller Design Model

Chapter IV and the accompanying exercises focus on three objective complexes. Using the clues provided in the parentheses below, thumb through the chapter and write your version of these complexes, (in behavioral terms)* in the space provided.

1. (Regarding the functional relationship between the modified taxonomy and the design model): The learner will:

2. (Regarding the use of the "filled" [where the comprehensive list of objectives for the unit has been inserted into the model] design model in structuring individual lessons): The learner will:

3. (Regarding the use of the "filled" [where the comprehensive list of transitional objectives for the unit has been inserted into the model] sub-model in structuring individual lessons): The learner will:

_____

*Note: It is not expected that the learner will state these objectives in the same way as the author. In this exercise he has the opportunity to apply the models freely to his unique situation and perspectives.

Listed below are the author's objective complexes for Chapter IV. You may use them to revise your objectives, to add to your objectives, or to replace your objectives. There is no reason why the learner cannot have objectives above and beyond those developed in the curriculum materials.

The learner will:

1. Assign to the cells of the design model the objectives derived by analyzing a unit objective complex based upon the modified taxonomy method.

2. Select the appropriate terminal objectives for specific lessons using the "filled" design model.

3. Select appropriate transitional objectives for specific lessons using the sub-model.

Chapter IV
Exercise II
The Drumheller Design Model

Transfer the objectives you developed in Chapter II, Exercise II, abbreviating when necessary, to the Design Model structure on the following page.

UNIT LEVEL OBJECTIVES

(3.0) _____
_____
_____

SUB-UNIT I	II Analysis	III Synthesis	IV Evaluation
	(4.1) _____	(5.1) _____	(6.1) _____
	(4.2) _____	(5.2) _____	
			(6.2) _____
	(4.3) SUB UNIT	(5.3) LEVEL OBJECTIVES	

(1.11) _____
(1.12) _____

(1.21) _____
(1.22) _____
(1.23) _____
(1.24) _____
(1.25) _____

(1.31) _____
(1.32) _____

RUDIMENTARY LEVEL OBJECTIVES

(Affective) _____
_____

(Psycho-Motor) _____
_____

Evaluation Suggestions:

1. The numbers in parentheses provide the keys for the transfer of the objectives. They refer to the taxonomy code.

2. Some rationales for the affective and psychomotor objectives are found in Chapter IV, page 34.

Chapter IV
Exercise III

Exercise III is different from the previous ones. It has been designed as a culminating activity because it provides insights into the way the Design Model functions to serve the writer and the teacher in their routine professional activities. In may be best if this exercise were developed cooperatively by pairs of teachers (see suggestions on page 103) who could strive to reach a consensus before recording their responses. The exercises can, however, be beneficial to one working alone.

1. List all of the terminal objectives appearing on the chart on the preceding page that would apply to the first lesson of Sub-Unit II. Remember that you listed only one of the possible objectives for each taxonomy category. If you find it necessary to list terminal objectives other than those found on the chart, put them in parentheses. (Consider only new material.)

2. List all the terminal objectives appearing on the chart on the preceding page that would apply to the first lesson of Sub-Unit III. (Consider only new material.)

3. List all the terminal objectives appearing on the chart on the preceding page that would apply to the first lesson of Sub-Unit IV. (Consider only new material.)

Evaluation Suggestions:

1. Sub-Unit II response: These objectives should focus on the introduction of the analysis skills needed to reach the terminal behaviors. Because analysis focuses on the identification of relevant knowledge components, these knowledge elements should also appear on your list.

2. Sub-Unit III response: These objectives should focus on the introduction of synthesis skills needed to reach the terminal behaviors. Because synthesis skills are dependent upon the learner's ability to select relevant knowledge referents with which he can build his synthesis, these knowledge elements should appear on your list.

3. Sub-Unit IV response: These objectives should focus on the introduction of the evaluation skills needed to reach the terminal behaviors. Because the evaluation process is dependent upon the learner's ability to use his knowledge of criteria, these knowledge elements (and possibly others) should appear on your list.

Chapter V
Exercise I

1. Using the Sub-Model on page 40, list the transitional objectives that would apply to the first lesson of Sub-Unit II. (You may add objectives not specified in the Sub-Model.)

2. Using the Sub-Model, list the transitional objectives that would apply to the first lesson of Sub-Unit III. (You may add objectives not specified in the Sub-Model.)

3. Using the Sub-Model, list the transitional objectives that would apply to the first lesson of Sub-Unit IV. (You may add objectives not specified in the Sub-Model.)

Evaluation Suggestions:

The transitional objectives focus on "means" and not "ends." The Sub-Model suggests some means, but the teacher (or the writer of curriculum materials) is left with the freedom to select transitional objectives at his own discretion. If your statements meet the criteria for good behavioral objectives, and you can defend them in terms of your methodology, they are acceptable.

Chapter V
Exercise II

1. Write the "procedure" portion of a plan for the first lesson of Sub-Unit II based upon the terminal and transitional objectives identified in Exercise III (Chapter IV) and Exercise I (Chapter V).

2. Write the "procedure" portion of a plan for the first lesson of Sub-Unit III based upon the terminal and transitional objectives identified in Exercise III (Chapter IV) and Exercise I (Chapter V.)

Adapting These Exercises for Use in Inservice Workshops

This book was designed to provide writers with an orientation that will enable them to work effectively as a team in developing curriculum materials according to a master plan. It was further hoped that teachers can use the approach as an orientation for developing curricula and materials appropriate to their local needs.

When a group must function as an organic unit to accomplish a curriculum task, it is necessary that they be oriented as a group. For example, if several teachers were to read this book and perform the exercises individually, it is likely that they would emerge with a variety of conflicting views and different understandings. On the other hand, if they discuss difficult points as a group at appropriate times, a consensus can be reached.

For this reason, the author favors a workshop approach to the mastery of the behaviors described in this guide book. The exercises on the preceding pages may also be used as small group discussion exercises.

Here are recommended procedures:

1. For use in classes where members will not again function as a group: The instructor will place learners in groups of two or three so that each group will consist of learners with similar subject and grade level interests. Regardless of whether the material is presented by an instructor or through this text, the exercises may be attacked in one of these ways:

   a. The learner will complete the exercise, in writing, without conferring with a group member. The group will then meet and prepare a new set of responses based upon a group consensus. In Exercise III (Chapter II) the group will first have to agree on the terminal objective before individual responses can be prepared.

   b. When time is at a premium, individual responses may be omitted. After learners have been exposed to the point of view, they proceed to prepare a group response to the exercise.

2. When it is desirable to develop a functioning group oriented to the design point of view: The instructor will form groups that will consist of members who have the talent, interest, and resources to perform the tasks with which the group ultimately will be confronted. Such a group can work effectively with as many as 12 to 15 members. When the group will stay together for an extended time, it may be wise to include a session or two of instruction and practice in group dynamics. Again, the exercises may be used in one of the two ways described above.

Appendix II

Foldout